E C C O
Travels

THE Spanish Temper

by V. S. Pritchett

THE ECCO PRESS

New York

To Dorothy

First published in 1989 by The Ecco Press
26 West 17th Street, New York, NY 10011
Published simultaneously in Canada by
Penguin Books Canada Ltd., Ontario
Printed in the United States of America

Library of Congress Cataloging-in-Publication Data

Pritchett, V. S. (Victor Sawdon), 1900–
   The Spanish temper.
   Includes index.
   1. National characteristics, Spanish.   I. Title.
DP52.P7   1989   828'.91203   88-36338

ISBN 0-88001-182-3

10 9 8 7 6 5 4 3 2 1

Introduction

The Spanish Temper was first published in 1954 and has often been reprinted. It was written after long experience of Spain going back thirty years. I was twenty-three when I first went there and I spent two years in Madrid as the correspondent of the *Christian Science Monitor* though scarcely trained as a journalist. I did not know the language or anything much about the country although, by some prophetic freak of childhood, I had written 100 pages of a novel about the fall of Granada when I was twelve. Fortunately there was little news to report under what now seems the amiable military dictatorship of Primo de Rivera, and I was encouraged to travel all over the country. In those days one went to Spain by train from Paris and I shall not forget that freezing winter day when I crossed the frontier at Hendaye and hours later had my first sight of the dreadful Pancarbo Pass up which the train crawled to the strange, moon-like tableland and the saw-edged mountains of Castile. That landscape excited my imagination; I longed to walk across it. And, in time, I did walk from Badajoz in the South to Vigo in the North West and in the then little known mountains of the Asturias. I heard for the first time what Borrow called 'the lordly language of Castile' and, in the next years I was deep in learning it, deep in Spanish history, Spanish literature and in the Spanish painters and in speculation about the Spanish nature.

And so, at once, I was captured. I was lucky to be in Spain at a time when most of the members of the famous 'generation of '98' were alive and in their middle years – Baroja and Ayala, the novelists; Azorin the graceful essayist; Unamuno and Ortega y Gasset, the philosophers; and many more who, after the disaster of Cuba, were out to arrest the backwardness of Spain by re-education. Among the poets were there Machado, Juan Ramon Jimenez and the young Lorca. Many of them took kindly to an earnest young foreigner and indeed re-educated *me*. They freed me of the crude northern notion of the so-called 'black legend' of Spanish fanaticism in religion and equally of the romantic illusions of Carmen's Spain of 'blood and bulls'. At the end of those two years it is not an exaggeration to say that Spain was my first university and that it had changed my life.

I am by second nature a passive rather than an offensive traveller: that is to say I was not inclined to the

The Spanish Temper

mocking views that many even very distinguished British and indeed French travellers have assumed in countries foreign to them. I was inclined rather to un-English or un-self myself. Spanish fanaticism was repellent to me, but what influences had created it? Were there not other strains in the Spanish nature or temper? In the end I certainly was not un-Englished, but I had met that enemy of the unexamined beliefs I had inherited; the enemy who becomes the indispensable friend when one is young and callow. When my job came to an end I was so captivated that I returned again and again to Spain until the Civil War, not as a holiday maker but to travel more, often very rough. In the Fifties, after that savage war – the third to occur in a hundred years – I returned again to write this book and repay the debt I owed to my Spanish mentors on both sides of their conflict, many of whom had been executed, imprisoned or had fled into exile. The Spain I knew had not quite gone, but it had entered the twentieth century, the last country in western Europe to do so. The peasantry had left the land in their hundreds of thousands: the cities now had massive modern suburbs. Huge apartment blocks now stood like fortifications round the old core; cars now crowded the once impassible roads along which the mule teams had straggled – even in the centre of Madrid they used to be entangled with the little yellow trams. Shabby cafés had become grandiose, the little fishing village of

Torremolinos had become like a huge chunk of California and little Malaga had now its daily pall of brown smog. The aeroplane had brought in mass tourism and the silent little streets of forgotten towns which had seen only an occasional professor were now packed with gaudy foreigners. The social changes and changes in custom were enormous, and my book is no guide to them, and certainly not to contemporary politics. It is clear there is a change in the status of women and that there are considerable changes in popular and advanced education. Yes, there has been some kind of social revolution: a people who once stuck fiercely to their regions have now been shaken out of them, as the British were shaken out of theirs by their own industrial revolution 150 years ago. Even so, to my ear and eye, the Spanish nature or temper does not seem to have been changed very much. The intense anarchic individualism still seems to prevail, and so does the inherent and striking manly dignity.

—V. S. PRITCHETT   *London, 1983*

Preface

This is a personal book and not primarily a work of information. It assumes the reader has at any rate read his Guide. I write because, of all the foreign countries I have known, Spain is the one that has made the strongest impression on me. I went there first in the 1920's as a very young man and lived there for nearly two years; the effects of the experience were drastic and permanent. I might almost say, without being guilty of rhetoric, that the sight of the landscape of Castile changed my life. It is not difficult to see why this should be so: I read Unamuno's *Del Sentimiento Trágico de la Vida*. But even had I not done so I would still have seen that Spain is the old and necessary enemy of the West. There we learn our history upside down and see life exposed to the skin. Neither in France nor in Italy can one be so frankly frightened. All the hungers of life are blankly stated there. We see the primitive hungers we live by and yet, by a curious feat of stoicism, fatalism, and lethargy, the passions of human nature are sceptically contained.

In variety, strangeness, and grandeur the Spanish landscape is unequalled in Europe. I went to live in Madrid in 1924, and in the next two years travelled in most parts of the country. I walked in the mountains of the Asturias, in the Gredos and the Guadarrama. Two years later I walked from Badajoz through Extremadura to Vigo, staying mainly in the villages of that region. The journey is described in a juvenile book, *Marching Spain*, now happily out of print. This was what now seems the happy period of Primo de Rivera. I went again several times until 1935, and by then the rising in the Asturias had occurred and the prisons were full; fanaticism on the Right and the Left was rapidly taking Spain into the Civil War. This war brought horror down upon the Spaniards and, for the foreigner, its deceptions and shames. Few of my Spanish friends took the simple view of Spanish history and society which was offered to them by the early stages of the anti-fascist struggle in Europe; quickly they were divided, many were murdered by one side or the other. While, on the one hand, the disgraceful swindle of Non-Intervention was being managed by the powers, and the British government abandoned their traditional Spanish policy and betrayed their friends, it also became clear, on the other hand, that

The Spanish Temper

Western ideologies were instinctively rejected by the Spaniards. Woe to the foreigner of any party who gets involved in the Spanish quarrel and who believes Spain is an extension of Europe.

I did not expect ever to go to Spain again after 1935, but the force of the original attraction was permanent. Curiosity was too strong and I went in 1951 and 1952 to find a country often greatly changed on the surface, overrun by tourists in the show places, poor in body, stunned in mind, but not, as it seems to me, fundamentally changed. These two journeys are the immediate basis of the present book. It contains many generalizations and observations which will be disputed, for Spaniards rarely agree about anything which is said about their country; but in so far as general statements can be made by a traveller, they will be found I think to have plenty of sources in Spanish literature and life. I owe many debts which are recorded in the text. I would especially draw the attention of those who are interested in the background of the Civil War to read Franz Borkenau's *The Spanish Cockpit*. I owe a great deal of the material relating to the economic background to my friend Gerald Brenan's two books: *The Spanish Labyrinth* and *The Face of Spain*. No one knows the country better than he does; no one is wiser and more illuminating about it.

V. S. PRITCHETT

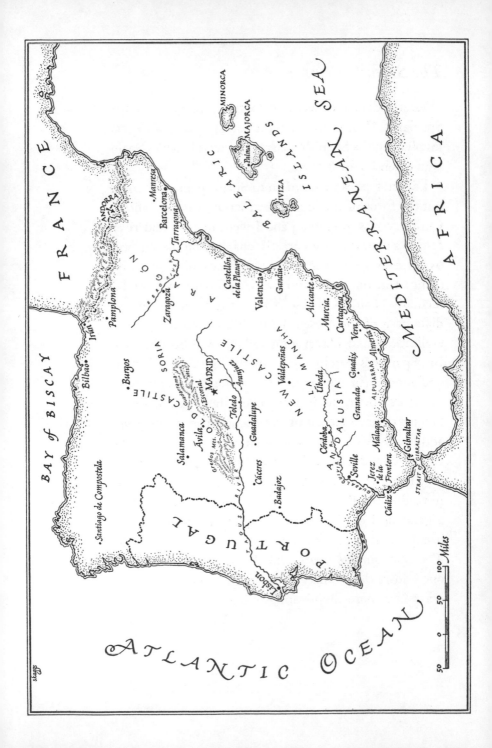

Chapter I

I make these notes during those two hours of impatience which begin in the early morning when the electric train clatters out of Biarritz Ville. One is hungry and queasy, one has slept badly and begins smoking nervously and too soon. In the corridor no one wants to talk after this night. Women are patching up their faces, combing their hair, men stand outside rubbing the night's growth of beard. The lavatory smells. One watches the long shadows of the rising sun in the pines; one sees the dust, the dewy greenness, the dry, heavily tiled houses, the fruitful green of a kind climate, a candid sky, and the sedate life. Yesterday's sun is still warm in these villa towns of terracotta. Here one would be glad to have a doll's house and count one's pension and *rentes* thirty times a day like a Frenchman and rest one's nervous northern mind in conversation consisting so largely of abstract nouns, to parcel out one's sous, one's pleasures and permissions.

But the prolonged sight of France annoys; one is impatient for the drama of the frontier and for the violent contrasts, the discontent and indifference of Spain. One is anxious to fill out that famous text of Galdós, so often quoted from the *Episodios Nacionales:* "O Spain, how thou art the same into whatsoever part of thy history one may look! And there is no disguise to cover thee, no mask to hide thy face, no fard to disfigure thee, for wherever thou appearest, thou art recognized at once from a hundred miles away, one half of thy face—fiesta; and the other misery; one hand bearing laurels and the other scratching thy leprous sores."

To know what we are up against we ought to go to Spain by aeroplane and fly to the centre of it. Beneath us England is packed with little houses, if the earth is visible at all through the haze; France lies clearly like green linoleum broken into a small busy pattern, a place of thriving little fields; but cross the dark blot of the Pyrenees, and Spain is reddish brown, yellow, and black, like some dusty bull restive in the

4

rock and the sand and (we would guess) uninhabited. The river-beds are wide and bleached and dry. After Switzerland this is the highest country in Europe. The centre is a tableland torn open by gorges, and on the table the mountain ranges are spaciously disposed. There is little green, except on the seaboard; or rather the green is the dark gloss of ilex, olive, and pine, which from the height at which we are flying appear in lake-like and purple blobs. For the most part we are looking down at steppe which is iced in the long winter and cindery like a furnace floor in the short summer. Fortified desert—and yet the animal image returns again and again in this metalled and rocky scene, for occasionally some peak will give a sudden upward thrust, like the twist of a bull's horns, at the wings of the plane. Flying over Spain, we wonder at the torture that time had put upon the earth's crust and how human beings can live there. In Soria, the terrible province, below the wicked mountains of Aragón I remember picking up an old woman who had fallen off her donkey and carrying her to the side of the road and wiping the blood off her nose. She was a figure carved in wood, as light as a husk. It was like having starvation in one's hands.

But it is better, I think, to go the slow way to Spain and to feel the break with Europe at the land frontiers. It is true that at Irún one is not in Spain but in the

Basque provinces, among people of mysterious race and language who are an anomaly in Europe; and that, at the other end of the Pyrenees, one is in Catalonia, where the people are really Provençal, speak their own tongue, and scornfully alter the Spanish proverb: "Africa begins at the Pyrenees," into "Africa begins at the Ebro." But the stamp of Spain is on these provinces and the Spanish stain runs over the frontiers. One finds it in Montpellier; on the Atlantic side it reaches into Biarritz, Saint-Jean-de-Luz, and Bayonne. And in these towns one meets something profoundly and disturbingly Spanish, which goes down to the roots of the Spanish nature: one meets the exiles. For, long before the Europe of the 1930's or the Russia of the early nineteenth century, Spain is the great producer of exiles, a country unable to tolerate its own people. The Moors, the Jews, the Protestants, the reformers—out with them; and out, at different periods, with the liberals, the atheists, the priests, the kings, the presidents, the generals, the socialists, the anarchists, fascists, and communists; out with the Right, out with the Left, out with every government. The fact recalls that cruel roar of abuse that goes up in the ring when the bullfighter misses a trick; out with him. Hendaye and Bayonne are there to remind us that before the dictatorships and police states and witch-hunters of contemporary history, Spain has been imperial in the trade of producing exiles. And the exiles go out over the bridge at Hendaye into France, the country that has tolerated all, and at the windows of the French hotel the new exile stands, looking across the bight of sea at the gloomy belfries of his native country, hears their harsh bells across the water, and hates the France which has given him sanctuary. He is proud of his hatred, sinks into fatalism, apathy, intrigue, quarrels with all the other exiles, and says with pride: "We are the impossible people."

Hendaye: the train dies in the customs. One gets a whiff of Spanish impossibility here. A young Spaniard is at the carriage window talking to a friend who is on the platform. The friend is not allowed on the platform; what mightn't he be smuggling? The gendarme tells him to go. The Spaniard notes this and says what he has to say to his friend. It is a simple matter.

"If you go over to see them on Wednesday tell them I have arrived and will come at the end of the week." But if a bossy French gendarme thinks that is how a Spaniard proceeds, he is wrong. The simple idea comes out in this fashion:

"Suppose you see them, tell them I am here, but if not, not; you may not actually see them, but talk to them, on the telephone perhaps, or send a message by someone else and if not on Wednesday, well then Tuesday or Monday, if you have the car you could run over and choose your day and say you saw me, you met me on the station, and I said, if you had some means of sending them a message or you saw them, that I might come over, on Friday, say, or Saturday at the end of the week, say Sunday. Or not. If I come there I come, but if not, we shall see, so that supposing you see them . . ." Two Spaniards can keep up this kind of thing for an hour; one has only to read their newspapers to see they are wrapped in a cocoon of prolixity. The French gendarme repeats that the Spaniard must leave. The Spaniard on the platform turns his whole body, not merely his head, and looks without rancour at the gendarme. The Spaniard is considering a most difficult notion—the existence of a personality other than his own. He turns back, for he has failed to be aware of anything more than a blur of opposition. It is not resented. Simply, he is incapable of doing more than one thing at a time. Turning to the speaker in the train, he goes over the same idea from his point of view, in the same detail, adding personal provisos and subclauses, until a kind of impenetrable web has been woven round both parties. They are aware of nothing but their individual selves, and the very detail of their talk is a method of defeating any awareness of each other. They are lost in the sound of their own humming, monotonous egos and only a bullet could wake them out of it. Spanish prolixity, the passion for self-perpetuating detail, is noticeable even in some of their considerable writers—in the novels of Galdós, for example: in the passage I have quoted there are three images to describe "disguise"— and it creates a soft impenetrable world of its own. Yet they have a laconic language, the third-person form of address is abrupt and economical, their poetry even at its most decorative is compressed in its phrases and cut down to the lapidary and proverbial, and they can be as reserved and silent as the English; and yet when, in their habit of going to extremes, they settle down to talk, one feels one is watching someone knitting, so fine is the detail, so repetitious the method. The fact is that they are people of excess: excessive in silence and reserve, excessive in speech when they suddenly fly into it. It is absurd of course to generalize about a nation from the sight of two people on a railway platform; but we are travellers—let us correct one generalization by adding a great many more. There will be time to reflect on the variety of human nature, and the sameness of its types, afterwards. Let us consider the other Spaniards on the train.

It was easy to pick them out from the French when they got on the train in Paris; not quite so easy to pick them out from the Italians. The Spanish men were better dressed than the other Latins, and this was true of all classes. Their clothes fitted them at the waist and the shoulders, they carried themselves with reserve and dignity. Their gestures were restrained, their farewells were quiet and manly, they did not talk much and what they said was dry, composed, and indifferent. They behaved with ease as people who live by custom do; and they gave an impression of an aristocratic detachment. This is true of all classes from the rich to the poor, who have the same speech and the same manners. There are no class accents in Spain worth mentioning; there are only the regional variants of speech. This man is an Andalusian, this a Gallego; you can only guess his class from his clothes. One is markedly among gentlemen, and even the "señorito," the bouncing little mister, falls back on that when he has exhausted his tricks. The word "gentleman" is not altogether complimentary, for it implies a continual conscious restraint on part of the human personality, and it carries a narrow connotation of class. In this narrow sense a Spaniard cannot be a "gentleman," for though he has a sense of fitness in his quiescent mood, he is unrestrained when he wakes up. His conduct is ruled by his personal pride, not by his category; and it is natural for him to be proud. His pride may be a nuisance, but it fits him and it cannot be removed. He is, he has always been, a hidalgo—a *hijo de algo*—a person of some consideration. And upon this consideration, however impalpable it may be, the very beg-

gar in the streets reposes. A point not to forget is that
in the sixteenth and seventeenth centuries the Spaniards were the master-race of the world, the founders
of the first great empire to succeed the Roman Empire,
more permanent in their conquest and administration
than the French, who followed them, successful where
the Germans have never yet succeeded, the true prede-
cessors of the British empire-makers of the eighteenth
and nineteenth centuries. The Spaniards in the train
had the simplicity of people who had once had the
imperial role. One could suppose them to be looking
back on it with philosophical resignation. The place
of those who have ceased to rule is to teach.

There was no conceit or vanity in these travellers.
The nervous pushing bustle of the European was not
in them. The quick vanity and sharp-mindedness of the
French, their speed in isolating and abstracting a problem, were not there. Nor were there the naïve vivacity
and affectability which electrify the agreeable Italians.
These races care to attract or please continuously; the
Spaniard cares very little and leaves to us to discover
him. He gives us time to breathe by his very negligence. "*Nada*—nothing," he says restfully before
every subject that is broached.

They stood in the corridor of the train and they
gazed at the fields of France. These fields are richer
and better cultivated than a good deal—though not

all—of the Spanish land. The Spaniard does not deny this, though he will think of the province of olives in Jaén, the *vega* of Granada, the vines of Rioja and Valdepeñas, and the long rich cultivations of Valencia and say, with that exaggeration which is natural to local pride, that these are "the richest places in the whole world"; and about Valencia he will be right. But Spain on the whole is a poor country, and he does not deny it. He is simply not interested in what is outside of Spain; because he has no feeling for the foreign thing and even regards its existence as inimical and an affront. He turns his back. His lack of curiosity amounts to a religion.

When I first crossed the frontier at Irún nearly thirty years ago, I remember listening to a declamation by a Spaniard against his own country. At the time I thought the protest was a sign of some specific political unrest, but I have heard that speech dozens of times since. Again and again: "It is one of the evils of Spain. We are decadent, priest-ridden, backward, barbarous, corrupt, ungovernable," etc., etc. Spain is either hell or heaven, a place for fury or ecstasy. Like Russians in the nineteenth century, the Spaniards are in the habit of breaking into denunciations of their country, and between 1898 and 1936 these denunciations culminated in a puritan renaissance. There had been two savage civil wars in that century and, among intellectuals, these wars presented themselves as a conflict between reactionary Catholicism and liberal Catholicism, between Africa and Europe, tradition and progress. In the writings of Ganivet, in Ortega y Gasset, Unamuno, the early Azorín, in Maeztu, in Ayala and Baroja—a brilliant school which has had no successors and which was contemporary with the effective efforts of Giner de los Ríos to create an educated minority—the examination of the Spanish sickness was made without rhetoric. Wherever one finds a superior mind in Spain it is certain to have been formed by this tragic generation, many of whom died of broken hearts in the Civil War, were executed, or are in exile. Possibly some of these train travellers have been influenced by them, possibly they are hostile or indifferent; if we are to find some common ground on which they stand we shall have to look beyond the accidents of opinion. That common ground is not their nationality.

For the Spaniards are not Spaniards first, if they are Spaniards in the end. The peninsula is a piece of rocky geography. It is the subject of Spanish rhetoric, the occasion for their talk about Spanishness, for chauvinism and rebellion—and they know from experience in every generation how those things end: they end in *nada*, nothing, resignation. The ground these travellers rest their lives on is something smaller than Spain. They are rooted in their region, even nowadays, after the Civil War, which has mixed up the population and broken so many ardently maintained barriers. They are Basques, Catalans, Galicians, Castilians, Andalusians, Valencians, Murcians, and so on, before they are Spaniards; and before they are men of these regions they are men of some town or village; and in that place, small or large, they think perfection lies—even the self-castigating people of Murcia, who say of themselves: "Between earth and sky nothing good in Murcia." One thinks of that little play of the Quintero brothers called *The Lady from Alfaqueque*. A lady in this lost little Andalusian town, who was so in love with it that she could be cajoled and swindled into any folly by anyone who said he came from that place. I remember a woman in Madrid who had spent the last ten years in political exile saying: "We had a much better life abroad when we were in exile, but I could never forget the water of Madrid and the craving for the taste of it became a torture."

This provinciality of the Spaniard is his true ground and passion. And with it runs a psychological parallel. His town is not like any other town. It is the only town. And he too is not like any other human being; he is indeed the only human being. If he is brought to the test, there is only himself in the world, himself and, at the other extreme, the Universe. Nothing between man and the Universe. For ourselves, the

The Spanish Temper

Westerners, there is something else besides man and the ultimate, or universal; there is civilization, or what Spaniards call despairingly *"ambiente";* and it is their continual argument that nothing can be done in Spain because of this "lack of *ambiente"* or lack of a favourable atmosphere; how can anything as mundane as a "favourable atmosphere" exist where people do not feel related to each other, but only to some remote personal extremity. The pious belong to God, not even to the city of God, but to some deeply felt invisible figure; the impious to some individual vision. In the end they are anarchists.

Irún. Holiday-makers on the French side of the river that divides the two sides of the Basque country watched the fighting begin in the Civil War here and saw men swim the river to safety. The town of Irún is famous in the history of Pyrenean smuggling. There have been two traditional kinds of smuggling on this frontier: the mule loaded with tobacco coming over the mountain paths at night, and the smuggling organized by high-up officials from Madrid, which is part of the bribery system that never dies in Spain. It is described in the Galdós novel *La de Bringas.* In all classes the personal approach through "influence" is preferred to the direct one; without "influence" one cannot "get in." A foreign official told me that after many years living in Spain he had come to the conclusion that there are two kinds of Spaniards: those who have "influence" and those too poor to have any; for the former, life is "normal," for the latter it is hell. The pursuit of "influence" is partly due to economic causes. In poor countries a job of some slight importance is a phenomenon and attracts a court of parasites. The fortunate slave at the desk is besieged by a crowd of less fortunate slaves; the fortunate slave himself is the unfortunate slave of one more fortunate. Like the Russian bureaucracy in Gogol's time, the Spanish is a huge collection of poor men. One has only to buy a motor-car or make a contract to be surrounded by people consumed by the anxiety to "facilitate" the deal, register the papers, put the thing through with the right officials, for a small commission. The affair would be lost in the ordinary and proper channels. Weeks and months would go by and nothing would happen. Fatal to take the normal course; indispensable to have an introduction in the right quarter. Watch the fortunate Spaniard at the railway office. Discreetly he inquires about a ticket, does not boldly ask for it. A significant rubbing together of thumb and forefinger takes place, a furtive flicker comes into the eyes. A little personal deal is starting: unfortunate Spaniards without "influence" will not get the seat, but he will. It is an unjust system, but one unjust flea has other unjust fleas on his back; the method introduces elaboration, sociability, a sea of acquaintance, into ordinary action: "I will give you a card to my uncle, who will arrange everything." Everyone in Spain, down to the extremely poor, to whom so little is possible, is waiting for someone else, for a "combination," or arrangement, of some kind, and since time is no object, they make a lot of friends. If time *is* an object, if it *is* a matter of life and death, then a black figure which all Spaniards understand, rises up and interposes her immovable hand—the great croupier, Fate. "*Ay, señor, que triste es la vida.*"

The railway station at Irún is as shabby as it was thirty years ago. The place is glum, thinly painted, and grubby. The eye notices how many ordinary things—things like pipes, trolleys, door handles—are broken. The grass grows out of the rusting tracks, the decaying old-fashioned coaches and wagons rot in the sidings, the woodwork exposed to a destructive climate. The railways were half ruined by the Civil War, but, except for the electric trains of the Basque provinces, they were always shabby and went from bad to worse as one travelled southwards or got off the main lines. After France this material deterioration is sudden except in one respect; in the last two years the Spaniards have built a new train, called the Talgo, which runs three days a week to Madrid and has

shortened the thirteen-hour journey across Castile by
two or three hours. This Talgo is a luxury, Pullman
train, low in build like the London tube coaches, and
each coach has a concertina-like section in the middle
which enables it to bend at the alarming mountain
curves in the Basque mountains. Its motion is, however, violent. One cracks one's head, or bruises one's
stomach against the handrails; but it is a change from
the slow, dusty, bumping caravan of coaches that
crawl to Madrid on other days of the week. Spanish
locomotives are always breaking down. There is still
not a complete double track from the frontier to Madrid, or from Madrid to Seville.

Nothing else has changed at Irún. One has heard
Spanish garrulity; now one meets for the first time
Spanish silence, disdain and reserve on its own soil.
Those superb Spanish customs officers, young, handsome, wearing the tropical uniforms of naval officers,
stroll up and down in a quiet ecstasy of satisfaction,
talking and aristocratically ignoring the crowd. Their
leisure is lovely to gaze at. The inferior officers who
examine your luggage wearing white gloves—it is
possible to refuse examination until the gloves are put
on, but I have never seen a Spanish customs official
without them—are poor devils and they get to work
suspiciously and tragically. They fumble with listless
dignity in the midst of some private wretchedness. The

tragedy is the habit of work, perhaps. They have the melancholy of people who go through this monotonous life with nothing on their minds, and not very much—at the present cost of living—in their stomachs. They look as though they are thinking of some other world, and possibly about death. More likely, until something dramatic happens, they are extinct. Our suitcases might be coffins.

Sombreness is so much the dominant aspect of these people that one is puzzled to know how the notion of a romantic and coloured Spain has come about.

What shall we declare at the customs? Almost everything will be opprobrious to them. We are English—and we have Gibraltar. We defeated the Germans and Italians; the Franco government supported them actively, and has in a large number of ways copied their regime. We are not Christians. By that the official means we are not Roman Catholics; if you are Protestant you are not a Christian. You are, for him and historically speaking, a Moor or a Jew. Or if we are Roman Catholics, Spanish Catholics will be quick to point out improprieties in our Catholicism. And then suppose you are on the Right politically, that will not help you. Are you a Carlist from Navarre, a descendent of those who supported the pretender to the Spanish throne in the two civil wars of the nineteenth century and who professed feudalism in politics and the ultramontane in religion? Or are you a monarchist, an old conservative, a clerical, a supporter of the Jesuits or the Army; are you *for* the Church *without* the Jesuits, or for Franco's Falange, which Franco himself does not much care for or, at any rate, plays down so that he can keep his balance between them, the higher Army officers, and the bishops? The Pope can be left out of it; the Spanish Catholics have always treated as equals with the Italian Pope. Or do you declare you are on the Left? Well, privately the customs officer is on the Left, or half his relations are. If you are on the Left you are a Red. But what kind of Red? Are you an old liberal republican, liberal monarchist, liberal anticlerical? One of several kinds of socialist? Which kind of anarchist? Which kind of Communist—Trotskyite, Titoist, Leninist, Stalinist? Though against the Church, are you a non-practising Catholic? A mystic? An atheist, a new atheist? The Spaniards are not allowed by government decree to discuss Party politics; there is only one Party. They do, of course, discuss them, but without much energy: that energy was exhausted in the Civil War, but the political look burns in the sad eye, a spark inviting to be blown on. And we have not exhausted the parties: for where do you stand on Basque and Catalan autonomy? Are you a centralist or a federalist?

The Spanish Temper

These silent questions are rhetorical, for, as I say, no political matters may be publicly discussed in Spain today. There is only one Party, General Franco is the conductor of a fractious political monologue. So exhausted is the nation by the Civil War that people have little desire to talk about politics. They have fallen back on a few jokes. And suppose that, hoping to curry favour, you declared that you were in favour of the state of vertical syndicates, the military conquest of Gibraltar and Portugal, the renewal of the Spanish Empire, the ecclesiastical control of all ideas, and a return to the glories of Fernando and Isabella, there would be an appalled suspicious silence. People would step back a yard or two from you and say: "Yes, yes, of course," and leave you firmly alone in your abnormal orthodoxy. For you would have declared something no Spaniard can possibly think: that the Spanish government is good.

But one does not make any of the foregoing declarations. One declares simply that, being a foreigner, one is inevitably the enemy; occasionally, in remote places, I have had showers of stones thrown at me when I walked into a village. I have been asked also whether I was a Portuguese jewel-smuggler in a place outside Badajoz. And, crossing the Tagus once, whether I was a Frenchman "making plans"—the tradition of the Napoleonic invasion still alive, handed down from father to son for a hundred and fifty years. And many times if I was a Christian, suggesting not that I was an atheist, but a Moor or a Jew. A Protestant is not a *"cristiano."*

I do not mean that enmity means open hostility; one meets that open, suspicious antagonism in France and Italy, but not in Spain, where manly welcome and maternal kindness, simple and generous, are always given to the traveller without desire for reward or wish to exploit. The poorer and simpler the people, the more sincere the welcome. In some lonely inn, a *venta* of Extremadura, where there are never beds to sleep in, but men sleep on the floor in the outer stables, while their mules and donkeys sleep inside, just as they did in the time of Cervantes, they will ask you if you have brought your sack and your straw, and if you have not brought them, they will get them for you. The suspicion common in industrial society, the rudeness of prosperous people, have not touched the Spaniards; one is treated like a noble among nobles. There is never avarice. One sits before the hearth, the brushwood blazes up, the iron pan splutters on the fire, and conversation goes on as it has always gone on. The enmity I speak of is part historical inheritance and part an unbridgeable difference of type. A very large number of the beliefs of people brought up in modern, urban, industrial civilization make no contact even

with the urban Spaniard. As for the historical inheritance, an Englishman thinks of the life-and-death struggle with Spain in the Elizabethan age. Spain threatened
our life as a nation, our Protestant faith, the idea of
freedom on which, for economic and spiritual reasons,
our life during the last four hundred years has pros-
pered. A Dutchman would make the same reflection.
To Protestants, Spain was what Protestants have hated
most: the totalitarian enemy. To Spanish Catholics,
the Protestant attack upon the Church was their supreme stimulus to action in the Counter-Reformation.
They were the first people in Europe to put into
practice ideals which liberal societies have always re-
sisted: the ferocious doctrine of racial purity or *"lim-
pieza,"* revived by the Nazis; the paralysing idea of
ideological rightness, the party line, supervised by the
Inquisition, which, for all the excuses that are made on
its behalf, remains the notorious model of contemporary persecution in Russia and in America. It was a
Spaniard who founded the first order of Commissars
in Europe, the Society of Jesus. Time has softened,
abolished, or transformed these things in Spain; but
they were, in spite, models which the enemies of liberal civilization have copied. The Spanish mind invented them and made them intolerably powerful.
They represent something which is permanent, still
potential, if not always powerful in Spanish life. One

may be a foreign Catholic and still be on one's guard against them; many great Spaniards have fought their country's tendency and suffered from its authoritarianism.

Spanish fanaticism has sown fanaticism on the other side of its frontiers. It has its comedies. How many foreigners, especially the English-speaking countries, are Ruskinians about Spain. In his autobiography *Et Præterita*, Ruskin describes his own ludicrous meeting with the daughters of his father's Spanish partner in the sherry trade, the Domecqs. He behaved with all the gaucheness and absurdity of a Protestant youth.

". . . my own shyness and unpresentableness were further stiffened, or rather sanded by a patriotic and Protestant conceit, which was tempered neither by politeness nor sympathy. . . . I endeavoured to entertain my Spanish-born, Paris-bred and Catholic-hearted mistress with my views upon the subjects of the Spanish Armada, the Battle of Waterloo and the doctrine of Transubstantiation."

The young ladies from Jérez de la Frontera would have only noticed his "shyness": shyness is incomprehensible to anyone born in Spain.

On their side, the Spaniards might reply, and many have: We are not an industrialized society, but look at the sickness of industrial man! We have little social conscience, but look at the self-mutilation of countries

24

that have it. If we are mediæval, the latest communities, and, most of all, the Communists, indicate a return to a mediæval conception of society. Whom would you sooner have, the Commissars or the Jesuits? We have digested all that long ago. Spanish scepticism is inseparable from Spanish faith, and though we have a large population of illiterate serfs, we have not a population of industrial slaves. We present to you a people who have rejected the modern world and have preserved freedoms that you have lost. We have preserved personality.

This silent dialogue in the Customs House is a dialogue of half-truths. It indicates only one thing: we have already been infected by the Spanish compulsion to see things in black and white. We are entering the country of "*todo o nada*"—all or nothing.

And change is slow. In the Customs House at Irún there is still that finger-marked hole in the station wall through which you push your passport; still that thin, sallow-faced man with the sick eyes, the shrunken chest, the poor bureaucrat's jacket, writing slowly in the large useless book, in silence. Thirty, twenty, fifteen, two years ago he was there. He wears a black shirt now, a dirty white shirt no longer—that is the only difference. He sits like a prisoner. His hands can only do one thing at a time. It is impossible for him to write in his book, blot his paper, and hand you your passport in a single continuous action. He certainly cannot hold passport in one hand and pen in the other. Each action is separate and he does not speak.

The Talgo fills up at San Sebastián with rich Madrid people returning from their summer holidays. There are dressed-up children in the care of nurses. Everyone very well dressed. In the whole journey, little conversation. A Brazilian like a little dragonfly tries to make people talk by extravagant South American means. He stands up in the passageway, but has few words of Spanish and only a phrase or two of atrocious French. So he suddenly begins snapping his thumbs above his head and dancing.

"Carmen Miranda," he sings out.

People turn their heads.

"Spain," he says. "Dance."

"Ta rara! Tarra," he sings dramatically.

People turn away and look understandingly at one another. "Brazilian," they say. Two distinguished Spanish ladies resume reading their two books on Court Life in the Reign of Louis XIV.

"Spain," sings out the Brazilian. "Bullfights." He begins to play an imaginary bull. The performance is a failure. This is the most decorous train in Europe. He sits down behind me and taps me on the shoulder.

"Commercial traveller?" he says.

"Almost," I say. "Journalist."

The Spanish Temper

"Me, the same. Novelist. Forty-seven novels. How many?"

"Three or four," I say.

"Come and see me at the Ritz." (He was unknown at the Ritz.)

This happy little waterfly had a demure wife who laughed quietly into her handkerchief all the time, in her pleasure with this exquisite husband. But the middle-class Spaniards—no. ("One does not know what class of person," etc., etc.) Anyway, it was impossible to talk to him, but one could have sung, I suppose.

The train drops through the Basque provinces into the province of Álava. It is Welsh-looking country of grey hills, glossy woods, and sparkling, brawling brown trout streams. The haycocks are small in the steep fields, the villages are neat and are packed round their churches. One sees the pelota court, and sometimes the game is played by the church wall. Pelota is a fast game, and the great players are a delight to watch as they hit the white ball and send it in a lovely long flight and with an entrancing snap to the wall. It is a game that brings out the character of the players and, although the Basques are reserved in most things, they show their feelings of rage, disgust, resentment, and shame when they fail in a stroke. Their audience does the same. Sometimes an excited shout of praise comes from the spectators, often shouts of bitter mockery, which are answered by glares of hatred from the silent player. There is loud betting on the games. The bookmakers stand shouting the odds on the side of the court and throw their betting slips in balls to the audience. There is pandemonium, cigarette smoke, the beautiful leaping and running of the white-trousered players, the tremendous swing of the shoulders as the arm flies back for the full force of the stroke.

The Basques are the oldest settled race in Europe. They are locked in their language. Are they a pocket of the original Iberians caught in the mountains? No one knows. Their language is like the code of a secret society and has been very useful to them in smuggling. Racial generalizations are pleasant to make but they rarely fit the case. One would suppose, for example, that the French and the Spanish Basques are alike, but in fact the French Basques are a poor and backward race of peasants and fishermen; the Spanish Basques are prosperous and those in the cities are active, well off, and progressive in the material sense. To a northerner they are more "progressive" than the people of Barcelona. When we notice that deterioration at Irún, what we are really looking at is not the Basque provinces, but the negligent stain of bureaucratic Spain seeping up by the railway from Castile.

28

The Spanish Temper

The traditional fanaticism of the Spanish Catholic is the expression of a people who are naturally prone to scepticism: they go from one extreme to the other. Spanish atheism is as violent and intolerant as Spanish piety. The Basques have a different character. Their Catholicism is solid in all classes and is not in the least fanatical. They have little religious superstition and have little regard—perhaps because they are poor in imagination and poetry—for the image-loving and decorative forms of Catholicism. Their religion is plain; their faith is immovable—*Qui dit Basque, dit Catholique*—and is married to the sense of tradition which rules them. In this they have the integration of primitive societies. That is to say their religion is racial and dispenses with both the aggressive and the mystical feeling of other kinds of Catholicism. In the Spanish Civil War the Basque Catholics fought for their autonomy beside the Republicans—the so-called "Reds," who were commonly anticlerical, when they were not irreligious—presumably because the Basques knew their religion could not be endangered. The Basque Christianity is closer to the Old Testament than to the New and is even a little Protestant in its plain, practical simplicity. The Basque novelist Pío Baroja, who speaks of himself as an anarchist and an atheist, goes as far as to question both the traditionalism and the religiosity of his people. He recalls the testimony of mediæval missionaries who found the Basques at that time completely pagan, and Ortega y Gasset has pointed out that in the Basque language there was no word for God. For this conception the Basques used a circumlocution: *el señor de lo alto*, the feudal lord higher up, the chief or the laird, a simple idea springing from their tribal organization and not from the religious imagination. The religious spirit of the Basques is exemplified by Saint Ignatius Loyola, the founder of the Jesuit order. Whatever may have been the visionary experiences of the saint, he thought of his mission in the practical terms of soldiery: the militant company obeying orders from someone "higher up." Elsewhere in Spain the Church has become separated from the people; in the Basque provinces it is united with them.

The Basques, like the Asturians and the people of Navarre, live in one of the satisfied areas of Spain— those coastal provinces of mild climate where the rainfall is regular and plentiful. They are either farmers on the family community system in which the property belongs to the family and the head of the family council decides on his successors among his children, or they are sharecroppers—and the success of this system lies in the liberal and reasonable spirit in which it has been worked. Yet every statement one makes about Spain has to be modified immediately. Navarre is a Basque province that has lost its language, and the Navarrese, shut up in their mountains, are in fact fanatical in religion and they are the main source of the ultramontane form of conservatism, called Carlism. Navarrese economy, too, is successful and prospers. But as the train travels south, the rainfall dwindles in Castile, the peasant farmer becomes poor; money, not crops, becomes the landowner's reward, the religious quarrel begins. We are among a different race of more dramatic, more egotistical, less reasonable men.

In the rest of Spain the Basque is thought of as insular, obstinate, reserved, and glum, a pedestrian and energetic fatalist, working in his fields, putting his steel-pointed goad into the oxen that plough his land, making the wines of Rioja and Bilbao, and smelting his iron ore; or he is thought of as a sardine fisherman and packer in those reeking little fishing towns of the coast where they stack the tins. These sea towns are clean, prim, dour places. There is a narrow gap between the headlands through which the Biscayan tide races into a scooped-out haven or lagoon—all harbours of the Bay of Biscay are like this, from Pasajes, near the frontier, to the mountain-bound harbours of Corunna. It is a coast that smells of Atlantic fish, the sky is billowy white and blue, or the soft sea rain comes out of it. Basques who can afford it drive out of the grey, warm, glum days towards Álava and Castile, to

breathe dry air and feel the sun, which reigns over the
rest of Spain like a visible and ferocious god. There
the Basque in his dark blue beret, which sits square on
his stolid forehead, is thought of as an oddity. His
family is matriarchal. The breaking of the marriage
bond is forbidden. Even the second marriages of
widows or widowers is disliked. Rodney Gallop, in
his scholarly book, *The Book of the Basques*, describes
the wedding night of a widow. The mockery was kept
up with the beating of tin cans, the ringing of bells,
and blowing of horns until sunrise. This custom is
called the *galarrotza* (night noise). It occurs, of
course, in many peasant countries.

My own collection of Basques contains indeed one
dour character: a man who ran a bar in France, one
of the exiles. He was a municipal employee and fought
against Franco in Bilbao. He was also obstinately
determined to visit his family there and did so twice
secretly. But money affairs cropped up. It was necessary to go to Bilbao openly. The matter proceeded
in the usual manner of the peninsula. First his relatives
used what "influence" they could find, working
through the relatives of relatives. He was told to come.
This was about five years ago and required courage,
for at that time there were tens of thousands of political prisoners; but in addition to courage this man had

the insurmountable Basque conscience. He fought (he told the authorities) because his conscience told him to do so; not necessarily for Basque autonomy, but simply because it was the duty of municipal employees to obey the lawful government. Such a conscience must have maddened and annoyed the Falange who had done just the opposite, but, for all their revengefulness and intolerance, the Spaniards recognize the man in their enemies, and when passions have fallen, maintain their dignity and seek for the *modus vivendi* in the same glance.

The other Basques I have known were Unamuno and Pío Baroja, the novelist. In Unamuno one saw the combativeness, the mischief and pugnacious humour of the Basques. A brief light of unforgettable charm, delicacy, and drollery touches their set faces. In Pío Baroja it is the same. I sat in his dark flat in Madrid and listened to the gentle, tired, clear voice of the very old man talking very much in the diffident, terse way of his books, watched the shy, sharp smile that never becomes a laugh, and the sly naïve manner.

"But who else painted your portrait, Don Pío?"

"Many people. Picasso, I believe, did one once."

"Picasso! Where is it?"

"Oh, I don't know. It may exist. Perhaps it got lost. It had no value."

As evasive as a peasant, but say anything against the Pope or the Jesuits and he is joking at once. I asked about the puritanical Archbishop of Seville.

"Never trust a Spanish archbishop when he behaves like an Englishman," Baroja says.

Baroja once signed the visitors' book in some place and where he was expected to add his profession, rank, or titles, wrote: A humble man and a tramp.

He sat at his plain oak table in an upright chair, in needy clothes and the same blue beret on his grey hair —it seemed to me—that he had worn twenty years ago when I first saw him. His eyes were pale blue, his face very white—one can imagine the baker's flour still on it, for he once ran a bakery with his brother. It is a sad sight, the old age of a writer who, in addition to the usual burdens, has to bear the affront of the Franco censorship, which refused to allow him to publish his book on the Civil War.

"They said it showed the Spanish character in a bad light. And that is true. We see now we are a nation of barbarians."

Baroja and Unamuno were broken by the Civil War. Baroja has fallen into melancholy. Unamuno, who came out on Franco's side as a good many liberals did, heard of the atrocities and rushed out into the streets of Salamanca screaming curses on Franco, the Falange, and his country, and went out of his mind.

The Spanish Temper

Baroja is an exceptional Basque in his hostility to the Church and in his anarchism; he has lived chiefly in Madrid. But he is thoroughly Basque in his obstinacy and his tenacity and his droll humour. Unamuno had the same obstinacy. His book *Del Sentimiento Trágico de la Vida—The Tragic Sense of Life*—is one of the most important works in the last fifty years of Spanish literature. He was the outstanding figure in the movement towards Europeanization, which began after the loss of Cuba in 1898, and he was all the more important because he embodied the ambiguity of the Spanish attitude to the modern world. The Basques live in prosperous and liberal-minded community; the rhetorical exaggerations and the desuetude of the rest of Spain are alien to them. They are, in fact, "modern" to a degree of modernity which not even the Catalans have attained. All the more, therefore, was Unamuno conscious of the need of Europe, all the more of the price. His life became a battleground for the quarrel between Reason and Faith, between the European consciousness and the mediæval soul. *The Tragic Sense of Life* sets out the essence of a profound conflict in the Spanish mind on its opening page, where he describes the subject of his book: not man in the abstract, but "the man of flesh and bone, who is born, suffers and dies—who, above all, dies and who does not wish to die."

Unamuno's book is a search for the solution to the problem which cannot be solved: man's agonized desire to be assured of personal immortality. We cannot have this assurance, but out of the agony our soul must found its energy. With its pugnacious egoism, and its Quixotic quality, Unamuno's philosophy described the positive side of the Spanish spirit, and came closer to the positive spirit of the Spaniards in the Counter-Reformation than their reactionary successors have done. There was more than a touch of the Protestant preacher in Unamuno, and the great figures of the Counter-Reformation were, in fact, counter-protestors who had not yet dulled and hardened into an oligarchy. Unamuno's energy and truculence, his nonconformity before the Castilian mind and authority, were very Basque.

Chapter II

None of this has been Spain, so far. Spain begins after Miranda del Ebro, where one sees the last big river of silver water and the last rain-washed, glass-enclosed balconies of the north. The train begins its climb on to the tableland of Castile, which occupies the centre of the country and which stretches east and west from Portugal to the mountains above Valencia and from the Ebro to the Andalusian valleys. The floor rises upwards of 1,500 feet above the sea—Madrid in the middle of it over 2,000 feet up—and it is crossed by saw-edged mountains which rise to 10,000 feet. The train enters the Pancorbo Pass, a place of

37

horror like all the Spanish passes, for the rock crowds in, comes down in precipitous, yellow shafts, and at the top has been tortured into frightening animal shapes by the climate. Nine months of winter, three of hell, is the proverbial description of Castilian weather, the weather of half of Spain: a dry climate of fine air under a brassy sun, where the cold wind is wicked and penetrating, a continual snake-fang flicker against the nostrils. Castile is a steppe. Its landscape is the pocked and cratered surface of the moon.

For myself, the passage through Pancorbo is the moment of conversion. Now one meets Spain, the indifferent enemy. Out of this clear, rare air the sun seems to strike, the senses become sharper, the heart and mind are excited, the spirit itself seems to clear itself of dreams and to dry out like the crumbling soil; one feels oneself invaded by the monotonous particularity of Spanish speech. It is a dry, harsh, stone-cracking tongue, a sort of desert Latin chipped off at the edges by its lisped consonants and dry-throated gutturals, its energetic "r's," but opened by its strong emphatic vowels. It is a noble tongue with a cynical parrot-like sound as it is spoken around one, but breaking out of this mutter into splendid emphasis. It is a language in which one hears each word, at any rate in Castile—in Andalusia whole sentences wash down the throat like the sound of water coming out of a bottle—and each word is as distinct and hard as a pebble. Castilian is above all a language which suggests masculinity, or at any rate it is more suited to the male voice than to the feminine voice, which, in Spain, shocks one by its lack of melody. Spaniards tell one that when they return from northern Europe, where the voices of women are melodious and sweet, they are shocked by the hard, metallic, or gritty, nasal voices of their Spanish women, and by the shouting pitch all Spaniards use.

On the steppe one is electrified, and one can feel one's life burn faster. Like the Spaniards, one sinks into torpor in the heat and one wakes out of it in flashes of intensity. So clear is the air, so hard the hard line of the horizon, that when the sun goes down, it seems to drop suddenly like a golden stone. The sun seems to be a separate thing, the sky a thing, the air a thing that can be felt in particular grains in the fingers or that can be caught, as even on windless days it keeps up its continual hard, wing-like flutter under the nose. In the green north all sights are bound together by mist, by the damp, and by greenness itself, and our minds dream on from one thing to another in a delicious vagueness, a compassionate blur; but in the south, and in Spain especially, there is no misting of the sights, everything is separate, everything is exposed, and there is no mercy extended from one sight to another. There is no illusion, no feeding of the imagination, and, in this sense, no perspective. The tree, the house, the tower, the wall stand equal in the sight.

Dust and yellow earth have begun; the grass, if there are patches of it, is wire, the trees only mark the roads, there are no others, and the roads, too, are rare. It is steppe, not desert, a steppe variegated only by wilderness. And there appear those strange flat-topped hills of the country. A half mile long, perhaps, and anything from 300 to 400 feet high, they have planed off at the summit and are water-hollowed in their flanks. They are as pale as china clay. Half a dozen of these dry hills would be a curiosity, like the Wiltshire barrows, but these mesetas stretch in their hundreds, miles deep like some geometry written on the land by wind and drought, an immense, wearying encampment. Some are pocked with tufts of grass: here and there some peasant has tried to cultivate a lower slope, but the water clearly drains off them and most of them are bare. No house or village is on them; they are the ghosts of nature and they pass in pointless fantasy.

These hills bleach the country and, in the heat, the air trembles over them. Their moment is the evening. When the sun goes down they are transfigured, for first they fall into lavender pools of shadow, then into deep blue and at last violet. For a moment or two the sight is weird and beautiful; then it becomes ghastly, for they take on the colour of bruised bodies, the corpse colour of those dead Christs the Spanish painters like to paint with the realism of the mortuary, the sick skin of the wrung-out stomachs and malodorous cheeks of El Greco's saints. The Spanish painters have dipped their brushes into the death-palette of the steppe, and that night change is one of the frightening sights of Europe.

Castile is a landscape of hidden villages, suddenly come upon, like crocks of earthenware in the soil, crumbling in the summer heat, sodden in the torrential rains of the winter; it is a place of sunsets in the haze of dust and of short twilights when the sky at the last moment goes green over the sharp violet mountains, which seem to have been cut out by a knife. The towns have no suburbs, but end abruptly in a mediæval wall or the long wall of some property. The landscape of Castile, Unamuno said, is for monotheism, not pantheism. God is a precise thing like a stone, the Christ is a real man bleeding, and the blood of His wounds stains the mother's cheeks as she leans against Him; the Virgin is a real girl. In this country the cemeteries are lonely, for they lie well out of the towns, with their enormous memorials, like small palaces. The black cypress marks the spot. Here if you die, you die. The peasants of these villages are like dethroned kings, grave in their speech, phlegmatic in their humour, with an irony as dry as Sancho Panza's, like the voice of the earth itself:

And so my master, these honours that your Grace would confer upon me as your servant and a follower of knight-errantry—which I am, being your Grace's squire—I would have you convert, if you will, into other things that will be of more profit and advantage to me; for though I hereby acknowledge them as duly received, I renounce them from this time forth until the end of the world. [Samuel Putnam's translation.]

If one stands on the edge of the meseta on the out-skirts of some place like Burgos, the first big town, the night comes down to one's feet. The loneliness is com-plete. There is the warm smell of the land and its pungent scrub, the trilling of the crickets as numerous as the large stars, which come so low in the plain that one might put out one's hand to touch them; and, to mark the human isolation, one hears the sound of some labourer tapping through the dust on his donkey and singing one of those songs which are made out of nothing and seem to have half Africa or half India in their melancholy fall, in those final "a's" and "o's" which drag on and break into smaller and smaller fragments of sound, till they vanish like sand:

"Era la noche de la fiesta-a-a-a-a."

All songs of desire and jealousy, the reminiscences of the casuistical details of passion. And it is not a night

42

of blackness, but of some dark and luminous substance: that dark silver one sees hanging like a body over Goya's *Dos de Mayo*. If El Greco painted out of the day and the land, Goya paints out of the night.

The hours are long in the sun in Castile. When the table-top hills fall back, one sees the small rivers in the yellow soil, and the miles of cornland where the mattock or the primitive, cattle-drawn plough has granulated the earth. For the steppe is not all desert; parts of it are wheat-bearing, and, like long, low white redoubts, walled in, as one would think, for defence, one sees the warehouses of the corn and the olive-oil companies. As in the Basque countries, the land is broken up in the northern parts—around Burgos for example—into small properties which are minutely divided among members of a family. Sons are what a man wants, though when he dies he may have to split his ground equally into patches of an acre or two, even divide one olive tree among all so that they may own no more than a branch each. In these parts the people are very poor, and one would expect to find that hatred of the Church and the landlords which is common in other poor parts. There is no hatred. Their small property, their mercilessly divided crops, make the peasants deeply conservative. And at night, in the harvest time, the back streets of Burgos roar with the shouts and quarrels of the wine-drinkers—a sound of drunkenness I have heard nowhere else in Spain, except in Andalusia, where they drink sherry by the dozen glasses; for outside of Burgos the Castilians are the soberest people in Europe. Only when one leaves Burgos well behind and when the average rainfall is even smaller does one meet the peasants who are hostile to landlord, moneylender, and Church.

And so Castile stretches towards its backbone, the Guadarrama and the Gredos mountains. There will be miles where the soil looks like stripes of red lead or ochre, distances of sulphur and tin, the sharp colours of incineration, as if great areas of the kingdom had been raked out of a furnace. As the train climbs to Santa Teresa's Ávila, there will be miles of wilderness where granite is piled up among the oaks or the short pines, and one sees the red fan of the partridge as it flies and the hunter standing with his horn and his gun. One feels lonely and free in the vast space of Castile, and the few roads suggest long, monotonous journeys. The eye picks up the green of the rare acacias or poplars which mark the metalled roads. On some mule track we mark the figure of some peasant riding away on a mule: miles between that figure and ourselves—who is he? What is the solitary insect thinking? What peasant with skin incised by wind and sun? We become absorbed, in these dawdling hours, in the task of overtaking a man who would greet one openly, talk in a pure, almost Biblical tongue, and who will speak his business straight out and expect to hear all yours.

"Good day. I am going to Santa X with this corn. I am from that village. There I have my family, my so many brothers, my so many sisters. Where do you come from? What country, what village? Where is England? Is that in France? Are you married? How many children have you? If you have, good; if you have not, bad. God has not granted them. What is your employment? How much do you earn? In your country"—the final deciding question—"is there plenty to eat?" And after that—some string of proverbs, a page of Don Quixote, a page of Sancho Panza. And then that lordly Spanish sentence of farewell and one's impression that one has been talking as a nobleman to a nobleman—as the Aragonese say, "We are as noble as the King but not as rich."

The egalitarianism of the Spaniards is not like the citizenship of the French, nor the anonymity of the English or American democracy, where we seek the lowest common denominator and try to hide our distinctions. The Spanish live in castes, but not in classes, and their equality—the only real equality I have met anywhere in the world—is in their sense of nobility or, rather, in the sense of the absolute quality of the person. One will hear this sentence spoken of people living in the lowest wretchedness: "They are noble people." These words are not especially a compliment, nor do they convey resignation, pity, or regret; they are meant, almost conventionally, to describe the normal condition of man.

If we were to travel with this man on the mule or donkey, we would not see his village until we were right upon it. It is some ruinous, dusty place, the colour of the soil it stands in, and most houses will be of a single storey. Only the fortress wall of its church will stand out, plainly buttressed high above the hut roofs of the village and built to last till the end of the world. It is the spire, the belfry, or the dome of the church that one sees first in the plain, rising inch by inch like a spear or a helmet, and it will give to the mind a lasting sense of a bare, military country, frugal and hard. In the wars of reconquest against the Moors, some of the churches—and cathedrals like Ávila— were built as forts, and of that time it has been said that the Spaniards did not know which they wanted most—the Kingdom of God or their own land. The centre of the village is a square of tottering stone arcades; the mule carts or the occasional lorry stand there. The inn, if there is one, will not be a hotel, nor even a *fonda*—the Arab word—but perhaps a *posada:* a place one can ride into with mule or donkey, where one can stable an animal and lie down oneself on a sack of straw, the other side of the stall. There are grand *posadas* like the Posada de la Sangre of Cervantes, which still exists in Toledo, places of heavily beamed roofs, and of courtyards upon which one may look down from the interior galleries; if the village is small enough there may only be a *venta* or tavern for the sale of wine and aguardiente. But there will be a ewer of water in the corner of the stone floor with a tin dipper in it, and that is what, in this dusty country, you make for. The water is cold and beautiful. Everyone praises its purity, and the man or woman staring at you with that prolonged and total Spanish stare will tell you soberly that this particular water is famous throughout the world as the best water on earth.

At nine o'clock at night they will ask you what you want to eat.

"What have you got?"

"Whatever the señor wishes."

And a Dutch auction begins. Meat, alas there isn't any; chicken, they regret; it comes down in the end to garlic soup and how many "pairs of eggs" can you eat, with a chunk of garlic sausage thrown in? They have "wonderful wine, the finest for miles"—but it turns out to be thin, vinegarish, and watered. The oil is rancid, but the stick fire blazes, the smoke fills the room, and there is war in your stomach that night unless you are used to the crude Spanish fry and to garlic as strong as acetylene. The food might turn out better than this of course; there might be bacalao, if you can eat dry salted cod; there might be pork off the black pigs; and resinous wine, scraping the top off your tongue, with flavour of the pine cask. They might catch and kill that screeching chicken in the yard or give you goat cheese and the close white bread which has come in again after the years of war and starvation. But good or bad, full or meagre, the meal will not be squalid or sluttish. There will be a piety and honourableness about it, no scrambling round the trough. The woman's hard voice will command the room and one will break one's bread with the dignity of a lean person who speaks of other things. "We give what we have"—not the "you eat the official portion which you're given or go without" of our sour democracies. They still—even after the Civil War, in which so much of Spanish custom died—turn to their neighbour before they eat and say: "Would you like this?" and even lift the plate.

"Please enjoy it yourself," is the reply.

Being so noble, they could (they convey) do without food altogether; or like the penniless starving lord in the picaresque tale of Lazarillo de Tormes, send in the starving servant to say: "Thank you, we have eaten already." Sober, frugal, austere is the Castilian living in these small towns that look like heaps of broken pottery in the plain.

Desert, cornland, wilderness of rock, mountains blade-sharp and bare, miles of umbrella pine near Valladolid, vines and white-walled towns south of the mountains, and richer oases of green: so are the two Castiles. A place of great castles visible for tens of miles, and a hard look of war upon a great deal of it. Spain is changing on top. The peasants are leaving the land, the population is multiplying, the cities like Madrid, Barcelona, Valencia, Granada, are doubling their size, and enormous, generally ugly, buildings are going up, turning Madrid and Valencia into suburbs of South America. The old Spain of the night watchmen who called out the hours through the night in towns like Ávila and Buitrago; of the scarlet-lined velvet cloak in Madrid and the scarlet uniforms, the *portero* with his lamp and javelin, the lover spread like a butterfly against the iron grille—all these have almost gone in the last twenty years. There has been a revolution. Certain things do not change. Castile has not ceased to be the unifying, the dominating force in the peninsula, the centre that holds the disparate parts together. What has Castile held together? The whole of Spain. It has forged the greatness of Spain in the sixteenth and seventeenth centuries; it has created the dominant Spanish character; it has written out in life the whole of the Spanish glory and the Spanish tragedy, what is superb and what is abominable in them. And Castile has created worlds outside of Spain. If Spain strikes the traveller as an exhausted country when he considers its political power or its institutions, a place where the vitality has been drained away from its public life and has flowed back into the people themselves, it is exhausted because it is one of the great mother countries in Europe, a founder of nations in the New World. Only the British have made a comparable expense of energy in the founding of nations, in the imposing of an order and a peace beyond themselves. The Spaniards and the British—and also the Portuguese—have far exceeded the French or the Dutch of the seventeenth and eighteenth centuries, and the short revolutionary aggression of France in Napoleonic times, in the pouring out of their vitality.

Thirty-one miles north-west of Madrid on a platform of the mountains three thousand feet up, stands the royal monastery, palace, and burial house of the Escorial, the supreme architectural symbol of Castilian ambition and its tragedy. The eye comes suddenly upon the monotonous prison-like façade, and the first pleasure which the sight of gravity and order give us, as they break the wild mountain scene and the grim wilderness of pine and boulder, quickly gives way to awe and melancholy before the cold statement of military power and the governing will. Built from the bluish granite of these mountains, so that it seems to be a projection of them, and coldly slated, the sombre establishment is one of the bare overstatements of the Castilian genius. Its thousands of windows stare and blink in the mountain light.

The Spanish genius is for excess, for excesses of austerity as well as excesses of sensual decoration. The soldier architect of the Escorial and the King, half-monk, half-bureaucrat, who built it, disdained the sunlight of the Renaissance and built their tomb in the shadow of the wild mountains and in the hard military spirit of the Counter-Reform. The Escorial is the mausoleum of Spanish power.

So it must seem to the foreign traveller, and most have been chilled if they have not been appalled by the sombreness of the place. To go there in the bitter Castilian winter when the snow is piled in the streets of the village and lids every one of the innumerable sills of the palace with white; to go when the wind bites, and when the halls, refectories, and chapels are dark, takes the heart out of the European. In the summer, when one gets out of the heat of the plain, the pine woods are cool and gracious and the palace is then grateful to the eye. The village has indeed become a week-end resort.

Yet calm, repose, or even that resignation which is exquisite to those who have learned obedience, are not suggested by the outward aspect of the Escorial. Outwardly it displays the platitudes of great power, and inside, though there are dignity and beautiful things, we are haunted by the melancholy of the founder, his morbidity, and the tragic quality of his faith and of his defeat. Here Philip II is said to have boasted that he ruled an empire from two inches of paper; here, like some bureaucrat, he tried to do all the work of the state, delegating nothing, devoid of the imagination or the gifts of his father, the Emperor—the prototype of the inadequate son who has been left an estate too large for him.

What were the estates that Philip II inherited from his father, the Emperor Charles V, who had come in with his crowds of Flemings to rule the country? There were the kingdoms of Sicily and Sardinia and Naples. There was Holland under the Spanish jackboot, brutalized by the Duke of Alba, ruled by the Inquisition. There was land in Africa and Northern Italy; and there were the Indies, which Columbus, Cortés, and Pizarro had added a century before. The largest empire on earth since the time of the Romans was the possession of the melancholy, uncertain, and mistrustful King who looked out of the windows of the Escorial and saw in his lifetime the beginnings of the Spanish disaster—the estate too great to manage, the stupendous act of will which cannot, in itself, sustain a nation for very long.

The Escorial is the oppressive monument to the first totalitarian state of Europe, for what distinguishes Spain in its short period of world power is its attempt to impose an idea upon the mind and soul of its own people and the people it conquered completely.

"He saw the deaths of almost all those whom he loved well, parents, children, wives, favourites, ministers, and servants of great importance"; Azorín quotes from Baltasar Porreño in *Una Hora de España*. "Great losses in the matter of his estates, bearing all these blows and trials with an equality of soul which astonished the world."

The Spanish effort to impose the Catholicism of the Counter-Reformation, to be the apostles and soldiers of the only truly reformed Catholic faith, to rule in that name, and to prevent by exhaustive means every deviation was a continuation in Europe of over six hundred years of war against the Moorish occupation. Spain has lived for long periods of its history in a condition of passive or active civil war, and behind the rubber stamp of the Escorial lies the history of a country struggling against its own natural anarchy. No Roman conception of law or citizenship, no Napoleonic notion of worldly glory and order, no English feeling that the self-interest of the individual must make a *mariage de convenance* with the self-interest of society, was strong enough in the Spaniards to control their natural anarchism—how much this simultaneous tendency to anarchism and despotism is a racial inheritance from the uncontrollable Iberians, and how far it has been formed in the long struggle with the Moors, no one can say. Their wars against the Moors encouraged the Spaniards to consider that they were cast for the part of the saviour who arises at great crises in history: they saved Europe from Islam, they spent themselves completely and forged themselves completely in this struggle. There was a psychological justice in it, too, for of all the European peoples the Spaniards—as descendants of the Iberians—were closest to the Moors they fought against.

The dark-skinned Berbers who crossed the straits of Gibraltar in 710 were barbarians, but, as wave followed wave in the following centuries, they built their own civilization in the rich lands and kind climate of Andalusia. They were conquerors—and it is now thought relatively few in number—whose aim was to exploit the Spaniards, not to assimilate them. Though many Spaniards became Mozarabs—or half Arabs—they were in the main treated as barbarians and they were disdainfully permitted to retain their religion and their customs. They were even allowed, in many places, to practise the Christian religion in the churches that had been turned into mosques. In some, the Jew worshipped Jehovah, the Moor Mahomet, and the Christian Christ, side by side. As the reconquest of Spain from the Moors gradually took place in centuries of continual guerrilla warfare, and in raids that grew into periodical campaigns, it was aided by the fact that Christianity had been allowed to exist in the Moorish territories. To the Spaniards, the war became religious before everything else, and by the time of the final conquest at the fall of Granada in the fifteenth century, the Spaniards knew themselves to be more Catholic than the semi-pagan Popes.

Six hundred years of foreign occupation and the wars against it had brought into existence three groups of people: the enemy, the conquerors, and those who had by force or in self-protection taken the colour of whatever side had become dominant in their region. There were Christians who became Moslem converts, there were Moslems who became Christian converts. There was the special category of the Jews. In their sense of crusade, in their drive for unity, the Spaniards began to imagine the internal enemy, the fifth-columnist or secret party man. The more they proclaimed unity, the more they suspected its absence. Purity of doctrine and of blood became an absolute demand. Was the Christianized Arab really Christian?

Was the Jewish convert really a secret Jew? And especially the Jew was suspect because, following his earlier persecution in Spain, he had sided with the Arabs and aided them in the conquest.

The Inquisition was the instrument by which the Spaniards sought to stamp out the doubtful and especially the Jews. They were deported from Spain in 1492 after years of violent pogrom.

The institutions of a world power like Spain are inevitably blackened by those who eventually break that power. Spanish absolutism, Spanish dominion, and its instruments were the natural enemies of the English and the French and certainly of all Protestant peoples. "The black legend" of Spanish fanaticism, cruelty, and rapid decadence is, to some small extent, the propaganda of the successful Protestant states. The Inquisition has become a byword in the world for the trial where there are no named accusers and no precise charges, and where confession is "spontaneous," where indeed confession is the only possible end; no question of guilt or innocence arises. It is the infamous model of all ideological tribunals. The Inquisition was the arch-destroyer of the free-minded, for though it began as a hunter-out of papistical traitors and false converts, it ended as a party instrument, so that—to hostile historians—the intellectual life of Spain was nipped off at every point when it could have flowered. No comparable institution outside of Spain was so intellectually relentless. The apologists of the Inquisition say that its terror and its burnings and imprisonments for heresy have been exaggerated. The Spaniards themselves do not seem to have thought there was anything abominable in it, and many have held that it preserved Spain from the witch-burnings and religious massacres of western Europe and was no worse, in the use of tortures and secrecy, than other tribunals of the period. Obviously the Holy Office had no immediate effect on the intellectual life of the nation, for the golden age of Spanish greatness in literature and the arts, as well as in political power, corresponded to the height of the Inquisition's authority. But the Inquisition was more papist than the Pope, and its corruption was an insidious social evil— "every sentence of death or imprisonment" carried with it the confiscation of goods which passed into the royal exchequer, the historian Altamira tells us, "but as part of them were paid to the functionaries of the Inquisition, they came, in practice, to be ceded to them as remuneration and this gave rise to great abuses." And the rigour of the oppression, this reliable historian pointed out, was very great at first. In the first *auto de fe* at Seville, he says, ten persons were condemned to death at the stake; "and, according to a contemporary, in the course of eight years 700 people suffered this fate and 5,000 were condemned to prison and other punishments." In Ávila, between 1490 and 1500, more than 113 persons were burnt. In one *auto de fe* alone, at Toledo, 1,200 accused appeared. In another, 750.

It is argued by the apologists of the Inquisition that, at any rate, it saved Spain from the slaughters of the religious wars in Europe; but Spain had been conducting what was essentially a religious war for centuries within its own borders and in Holland. How can historians weigh up these deaths in the balance? There is not the evidence available.

We can only repeat that the vigour of the Spaniards was exhausted in the pursuit of unity and religion, and they had no regard for the price. In expelling the Jews in the name of the purity of the faith and nation, the Spaniards performed a characteristic act of quixotry and idealism. They banished the practical and rational elements in the country. A million and a half settled people were replaced, Marcu says in *The Expulsion of the Jews from Spain*, by 300,000 adventurers who poured into the country to exploit it. Lacking the Jewish advisers and bankers who had held high office, the Spaniards fell into the hands of a foreign race famous for their avarice: the bankers of Genoa. The Genoese administered the estates of the grandees who had before employed converted Jews as their agents, and the Genoese did not keep their wealth in the country as the Jews had done, but sent it out. Marcu quotes a Spaniard of the period as saying: "Three hundred and sixty thousand foreigners in Castile have completely driven the Spaniards out of trade . . . without them we are unable to clothe ourselves, for without them we have neither linen nor cloth, without them we are unable to write, for we have no paper." The Spaniards who had become, by centuries of war, the knights of the new order and the purified faith, the superb conquistadors who founded the nations of America, had by a tragic retribution unfitted themselves for the rational tasks of civilization. They could conquer, win treasure, keep the faith, but not work. The humanism of the Renaissance had seemed weakness to them, the rebellion of the Reformation had seemed impiety—though it resembled their own effort to reform a pagan Church. They fought to preserve, and for a long time successfully preserved, the spirit of the Middle Ages. It was their triumph, their distinction, and their tragedy.

The Escorial is the tombstone of an achievement. It was in this mortuary that Philip II heard the news of the defeat of the Armada, which marked the end of his total power, and the end of an epoch in the history of the world. It was from the Escorial that this envious, suspicious, and cultivated man chose his leaders, as if to spite them. The Duke of Medina Sidonia had protested, when he was given command of the Armada, that he had no experience of the sea. It was from the Escorial that Philip, though the theologians had asked him to allow religious freedom in Flanders, had insisted that he would not dishonour God by ruling over heretics and that they must be exterminated; and fearing, every year more, the contagion of foreign ideas and the sin they would contain, closed the universities. In his book *The Spaniards in Their History*, the historian Ramón Menéndez Pidal says that Philip used means out of all proportion to the need, in his steps to preserve Spanish unity:

In the early years of his reign in 1558, Philip II prohibited under penalty of death and confiscation, the importation and publication of books without a licence from the State Council, lest those books might contain heresies, newfangled notions against the faith, or "vain matters," that might give evil example. Let us note how the penalty had increased, for in 1502 it only consisted in a fine and disqualification. In the following year, 1559, Philip II also disqualified Spaniards from studying abroad, except at Rome, Naples or Coimbra, or the Spanish college at Bologna. He gave two reasons for these restrictions: first because Spanish universities "are daily diminishing and in bankruptcy," that is to say he took the absence of the students as a cause, whereas it was only an effect of the bad state in which the Spanish universities found themselves. The second reason was that the intercourse with foreigners involved the students in extravagance, dangers, and distractions. And so as he did not find in the world any universities free from dangers except those at home or practically at home, he closed the doors and windows of the decayed Spanish schools so that the inmates might breathe nothing but their own confined air.

What is so hard to realize is that, to Spaniards, this policy of negation must have seemed positive, progressive, and the very expression of Spanish enlightenment at the height of its power. It was an assertion on the part of the richest, most powerful and vital country in the world of the sacredness and superiority of "the Spanish way of life." To ourselves, the heirs of liberal civilization, the policy of Philip appears as the irrevocable step backward. If Philip heard the news of the defeat of the Armada at the Escorial, his people were already creating a great Empire overseas. It was the exhaustion of their impulse, rather than anything we can moralize about, that was fatal. It is only peoples (we reflect) who lack deep unity who will put such fatal emphasis upon it and who will corrupt the idea of unity and make it uniformity; and when we turn from the Spanish idea to the Spanish reality, as far as we can pick it up from commentators of the time, we see the anarchy in which Spain really lived. Azorín in *An Hour of Spain* quotes the historian Cánovas del Castillo:

61

But in accepting this unity, each district remained as it was, with unchanged customs, with its own character, its own laws, its traditions, varying or opposed. Nor was even the footing of all the states equal: there were some of more or less noble standing, more or less privileged; some free, and some almost enslaved; for the Union had been carried out with very diverse motives, some districts coming into it voluntarily, as the Vascongadas claim to have done; others through matrimony, like Castile and León, Aragón and Catalonia; some through force of arms like Valencia and Granada, still populated by Moors; some half by way of justice, half by force, such as Navarre. And not only so, but even within the province every town had its code, every class its law. In this way Spain represented a chaos of rights and obligations, of customs, privileges, and exemptions, easier to conceive than to analyse or reduce to order.

"The perpetual tumult of opposing passions," says Azorín—that is Spanish history. Confederations, tribunals, committees. Cities rebel, juntas are formed, the fever spreads, the government is cut off. Citizen militias were created by the parties in the nineteenth century, as they had been in the time of the Catholic kings. The ashen façade of the Escorial, its bureaucratic frown, its appearance as of an infantry regiment drawn up in stone in the mountains, is the sign of an attempt to meet individualism, anarchism, and chaos by an iron and absolute power. Between the extremes the Spanish character swings.

The Spanish Temper

The Castilians, indeed the Spaniards generally, one might say, are people who are one thing or the other, black or white, as if there were a failure to connect between their senses and their intelligence. They are fatalists, yet they swing to the belief in free-will; that is, they are resigned to the law that is imposed on them or they reject it, suffer it, or combat it—nothing in between. Conquered they are fatalistic; victorious they are for extreme free-will. They have the bull's indolence, the bull's total courage and blindness in the charge. They are equal because they are comrades in arms. Their loyalty is to the chief. He is absolute and he rules by ordinance and *pronunciamiento*. These declarations stamp them, integrate them, pull them together, have the authority of a military order—and then, like old soldiers, they have their escape in the famous Spanish saying: *"Se obedece, pero no se cumple"*—"We obey the order, but we do not fulfil it or carry it out."

The Romans described the Spaniards as people adapted for abstinence and toil, for hard and rigid sobriety, a heedlessness of comfort, as indeed may be seen in their houses. They are born disciples of Seneca, natural stoics who bear and forbear.

"This shows itself," says Menéndez Pidal, "in the general tenor of their life, with its simplicity, dignity even in the humblest classes, and strong family ties.

The Spanish people preserve these deep natural qualities unimpaired as a kind of human reserve, whereas
other races who are more tainted by the luxuries of
civilization find themselves constantly threatened by
a process of wear and tear which saps their strength."

The Spaniards resist the pressure, this writer says,
of material necessity, and he contrasts Columbus, the
Genoese, the calculator and procrastinator who post-
poned his voyage until he had secured the promise of
enormous rewards, with the "host of Spanish explorers
despising material advantage," who went recklessly
forward gambling on their gains. The Spaniard is
arrogant and self-confident, despises the patient fol-
lowing-up of activity, despises foresight. In the
Escorial, Philip II solved the cost of the wars of the
Counter-Reformation by borrowing from the Genoese
bankers, never made allocations from one year to the
next, and lived for the day, meeting each difficulty as
it came along.

The Escorial is a monastery, the house of the dead
God who hangs on the Cross or lies on the earth beside it. The sense of martyrdom and death can hardly
have been more starkly conveyed by any edifice. It is
a stone statement of the end. In it is the mausoleum of
the Spanish kings, a chamber for the caskets of the
monarchs, a chamber for the caskets of the princes,
and empty caskets awaiting those yet to die. The new

king in the days of the monarchy saw his future resting-place. To the traveller, Philip II has seemed the horrifying personification of a death morbidly longed for. One sees the couch brought down to the corner from which he could gaze every day at the high altar, a shrivelled bald man with all the crimes of a great empire on his head, a man now covered with ulcers, swollen in arms and legs by gout, rotting with gangrene. Few people attended him, for few indeed could stand the stench.

"I had meant to spare you this scene," he said after he had taken the sacrament, "but I wish you to see how the monarchies of the earth end."

One walks out into the peace of the little town of the Escorial and smells the thyme and the lavender of the buzzing wilderness; one meets again the immense Spanish light. One will never be able to take that clarity for granted, for it is a material presence in itself. Light, which in the north is thought of as something relative, as an arrangement of varying degrees of shadow, a changing and filtering of colour, and which has no definition, is here positive and absolute. In the hot weather the tableland is like some lake or sea on fire; in the cold weather the light goes up higher than any light we know and transmits the sight to distances our eyes are not accustomed to. Above all, since it brings so much more of the world to our eyes, it has the effect of a tremendous accession of the sense of life. Here most earthily and most powerfully one feels oneself alive. Yet here one is confronted (and above all at the Escorial) with the Spanish preoccupation with death. No other race in Europe has this consuming preoccupation; where it has appeared in the German culture or in the addicts of the funerary urn and the skull in the English seventeenth century, it has been a passing mood. In Spanish life and art the preoccupation is continuous. *¡Viva la muerte!* was the slogan of the Falangists in the Civil War, and bloody pictures of the death of Manolete, the bullfighter, may be seen in the bars off the Puerta del Sol. The popular signs of the cult of death are as noticeable as the more sumptuous. One recalls the black-plumed horses of the ornate death coaches that move up the Castellana in the Madrid winter, the balconies and doorways hung with black cloths and sashes, the houses that are sombrely decorated for a period of mourning, not for the mere day of the funeral alone. Death, too, is a fiesta. In this cult no doubt some of the Spanish love of state and pomp and spectacle has its part. What contemporary foreigners could not but observe in the *autos de fe* was the solemnity of the occasion: the whole pomp of court and state displayed in person at the burnings. In Spanish painting and sculpture the theme of death is treated again and again by every artist. The gloom of the mortuary, the luxury of a lying-in-state, is their favourite subject. The preoccupation is common in Catholic art, but no Catholic artists in other countries have had so exclusive a passion; it appears also in non-religious painting. Goya's pictures of the terror and madness of war owe their dramatic force not only to the carnal realism, but to the sense of the life-and-death struggle, to the sense of life corroded at the height of its contest by mortal decay. In how many ways (Goya seems to have asked himself) can human beings be shown meeting their death? In Toledo, in the Church of San Tomé, we shall find the supreme expression of this emotion; in El Greco's *The Burial of Count Orgaz.*[1] It is contemporary with Philip II. The body is lowered into the grave, the grandees of Spain stand stiffly by. They are literal portraits of a ruling caste, proud, ascetic in appearance, their minds turned away from this world in a satisfied contemplation of the next; and some have seen in this picture the

---

[1] This famous picture was painted by El Greco in the last years of the reign of Philip II, and Cossío calls it "one of the truest pictures of the history of Spain" and of what Spanish society was like in body and in soul. The picture commemorates the death of a famous citizen, Don Gonzalo Ruya de Toledo, who was buried in 1323. He had built the Church of San Tomé in Toledo, and at his funeral the mourners at the grave were not astonished to see him carried up to heaven by Saint Stephen. The portraits are all taken from people contemporary with El Greco; the group is a gathering of neurotic gentlemen who have the air of monks. Cossío comments on "the cold and monotonous sobriety of its grey tones, its sharp spiritual note, its energetic expression of the national life."

67

idea of the living death of a caste, the suggestion of a racial suicide. They will rule in the Kingdom of God; we must neglect this life and hunger for death and the life to come.

Some writers have seen a mystical conjunction of voluptuousness and death in the nature of Spaniards. To Unamuno in *The Tragic Sense of Life*, the human tragedy was a passion: the sensual man of flesh and bone is born and will die, but there is planted in his mind the desire for immortality. In every moment of his life, he is living out this intense and dramatic agony. The sense of death is a continuous presence, as a fact and not as the shadow of a fear, and is therefore as intense as the sense of life. Man—for this Spanish egotist—must live out his life in absolute terms. Once more (one reflects) the preoccupation with death shows us the Spanish desire to see everything and live everything in black and white. Like Tolstoy, the Spanish egotist cries out: "What is Truth if a man dies?" But Tolstoy expected an answer; the Spaniard does not.

The foreigner need not think the strangeness of Spanish life has deceived him on this point. Menéndez Pidal directs us to the writings of Jorge Manrique, a Knight of the Order of Santiago in the fifteenth century, who describes three phases of life: the temporal life of the body, the life of fame, which is more enduring, and then eternal life, which is the crown.

"Now, these two lives after death," Menéndez Pidal says, "are as consciously felt by the Spaniard today as in the past, and so intense is his awareness that it contrasts with the attitude of neighbouring races. . . . The thought of death, which is thirst for immortality, is the profound concern of the Spanish people."

It is the individualist's thirst for a freedom that is absolute.

Chapter III

We have gone on too fast. Back over the Guadarrama Mountains the long-horned oxen graze in the scrub, those oxen whom the peasant guides not by a fierce stab of the goad in the Basque fashion, but by a gentle touch from the tip of the whip. The deep ox-bell and the small tinkle of the goat-bells are the sounds of the silent Guadarrama. One climbs through miles of pine shade where the lizards run; in the spring one sees patches of tiny daffodils, and will step across the sinister processions of caterpillars as fat as one's finger, that crawl head to tail in strings a quarter of a mile long. Wild dogs and wolves are sometimes met in these savage mountains. Over the top one descends to Ávila in its wilderness of rock. So gigantic and strange are the up-ended boulders of this wilderness, so thick the scrub where the large red Spanish partridge flies, that the eye at first misses the town which Philip II loved, where Torquemada has his tomb and where Santa Teresa was born. Then presently one's eye catches the perfect ring of mediæval towers and battlements which still contain the greater part of the town. They are like a great crown of granite in the wilderness and stand up against the hard violet wall of the Guadarrama and the Gredos mountains. Cold for half the year, burned by the sun in the terrible Castilian summer, Ávila is a plateau town, four thousand feet above the sea.

The spirit of Castile is austere, frugal, and inhibited. It is puritan and grave. The greatness of Ávila is in the sixteenth century; after that, it is the old story of sudden disastrous decline until now it is a lifeless provincial place. At Mass one stands in one of the packed churches and will hear the priest rattle off, in that loud, nasal, disparaging hurry of the Spanish clergy, a sort of guidebook lecture on the journeys of Santa Teresa. The glory has been reduced to a mechanical repetition, suited to dull people. In his reminiscences, *Places and People* (New York: Charles Scribner's Sons; 1944–5), Santayana has described what life was like in the late nineteenth century, when he was a child there, and later when he was a grown man, in the twentieth:

The place in my time was in part ruinous and neglected, reduced to 6000 inhabitants from the 30,000 it is said to have had in its day. Almost half the area that slopes down to the river from what might be called the upper town was deserted within its circle of battlements and towers; then appeared heaps of rubbish, a few nondescript huts, and some enclosures where occasional stray pigs and poultry might be encountered. Even in the upper part many old mansions and chapels were closed; sometimes only the great door, with a wrought iron balcony over it, attested their ancient dignity. Yet dignity was not absent from the good people that remained, leading a simple, serious, monotonous provincial life, narrowed by poverty and overhung, more obviously than busier places seem to be, by the shadow of illness, sorrow and death. Almost all the women appeared to be in mourning and the older men also: people were simply resigned to the realities of mother nature and of human nature; and in its simplicity their existence was deeply civilised, not by modern conveniences but by moral tradition. "It's the custom," they would explain half apologetically, half proudly to the stranger when any little ceremony or courtesy was mentioned peculiar to the place. If things were not the custom, what reason could there be for doing them?

Santayana did not believe that the people of Ávila had, at bottom, very much respect for their conventions or even their religion. Yet by bowing to custom, he says, their want "could preserve its dignity." It is that quality, uncommon in freer civilizations, that attracts us to the Spaniards.

The smells of Ávila are the aromatic smell of the wilderness which comes into every street, the reek of frying oil, or the cold sour smell of polish and charcoal in its stone doorways, of urine and excrement in the ruins, of the black pigs driven in at the great stone gates in the evening.

But the sense of being in a fortress—if nowadays only a fortress against sun and wind—is dominant in Ávila, for the walls are so strong and have lasted. As always, it is driven home to one that the Spaniards are the great builders of Europe, the true heirs of the Romans. No place brings home so dramatically the fact of the nearness of war to the men and women of the golden age. What—with our hindsight—we can see as the disastrous triumph of reaction, to them was the crest of positive and expansive action. When Santa Teresa was born, in 1515, Ávila was a place of fifteen churches. Her family's house was in the Jewish quarter of the town—a new biographer has suggested there may have been Jewish blood in the family—and, only twenty-three years before, the nation had enthusiastically and confidently expelled the Jews from Spain. She must have heard that Jews had been burned just outside the town by Torquemada's orders; her father's

73

family had fought against the Moors, and for a generation after the final defeat of the Moors in Granada, in
1492, all Spaniards feared a new invasion from Africa
as an act of revenge. When the people of Ávila feared
for the Christian religion, they saw in their mind's eye
physical enemies. The Jew or the *morisco* might be
the traitor burrowing from within. Yet the fear was
not defensive; it had an aggressive, idealistic, and re-
forming spirit. But to reform was dangerous. Were
the Protestants not reformers? Was not the Inquisition
there to question every act, to test its ideological
purity? In all the Spanish lives of that time one sees the
war of the spirit, with its open and its secret battles,
succeeding the victories of physical warfare. Yet in
her own lifetime Santa Teresa must have seen the fatal
decline. Those empty Jewish and Moorish houses must
have already indicated the disaster in work, craftsman-
ship, and trade. Over 11,000 Jews it is said left Ávila
in 1492, though perhaps that figure refers to the
province, not the town. If the town, it must have
meant not much under half the population. Whether
for province or town, the disturbance caused to economic life must have been violent.

Philip II, Saint Ignatius Loyola, Cervantes, they are
all soldiers—and their lives run with Santa Teresa's.
Santa Teresa herself wished for the liberty of a man,
and longed to go off as her brothers had done to the

74

new conquest of America. She told her nuns to regard themselves as soldiers. The interesting thing is the effect of the romances of chivalry upon the ruler and the two saints. When he wrote *Don Quixote*, Cervantes was not mocking some bookish old gentleman with eccentric literary habits. Don Quixote was reading what everyone who could read did read. The chivalry he described, praising its nobility and mocking its pedantries and magical wonders, was out of date, yet it occupied the common imagination. Santa Teresa read the romances eagerly when she was a child, and they roused the desire for brave action in her; Loyola read them at the time of the crisis of his life. We can say that these two lives were an adaptation of the romance of chivalry to practical use. Many writers have perceived the analogy between the Spanish resurgence at the time of the Counter-Reformation and the tragedy of Don Quixote, and, indeed, his book has been called, rather wildly, the book that killed a nation. When Cervantes came home, maimed at the Battle of Lepanto, and from his prison in Algiers, he too was a man who had made the knightly effort and who experienced the disillusion. The deeply sceptical Spanish spirit in that book arrives at its scepticism only after the plunge into intense experience. There can be no Sancho Panza unless Don Quixote goes out into the world of shadows. I do not mean that Don Quixote is conscious allegory, for it goes far beyond the Spanish situation in its time; it goes into the tragedy of the human imagination, carries it from the noble to the absurd, from the fantastic to the twilight of madness.

The great period of Mount Carmel, the religious house of Santa Teresa, was brief; less than a decade. What has survived is Santa Teresa herself: a woman gracious, positive, practical, and sober, not very imaginative, but of delightful poetic intuition. It is a character that survives. With Loyola the case is very different. From Luther, the Reformation; from Loyola, the Counter-Reformation, the Company of Jesus, and the Jesuit victory at the Council of Trent. From Luther the sectaries and their freedom, from Loyola the new ubiquitous commissars of totalitarian religion, the great explorers, the educators, powerful and mistrusted. To Teresa the soul was a garden; there was the will to purify but not the will to great power.

Jesuitism is European, the fruit first of Loyola's journeys outside of Spain; then of the transformation of his teachings by the Italian Jesuits, who introduced Machiavelli's doctrines into religious strategy. Machiavelli's error, they said, was in conceiving the political Prince; the only proper application was to religion— that is, to the greater glory of God.

Loyola belongs to the earlier, heroic and chivalrous time: well-born, first a page at court and then a handsome soldier and gallant, proud of his effect on women, brave in fight, and rich. He also added to these qualities subtlety and astuteness. The decisive crisis of his life occurred in battle. Both legs were broken by a missile in the siege of Pamplona, and he was left a cripple. This was a terrible blow to the great vanity he had in his physical appearance. He was tortured by the thought of being ridiculed for his limp, and he had the will and courage to make the surgeons break his legs a second time in order to make the cure complete. It was not, for he still limped, but his vanity was appeased.

For months he lay in bed, idle and dreading the loss of his life of pleasure, his love affairs, and his career as a soldier, and in this period he started to read the popular romances of chivalry. Amadis, the hero of Don Quixote, became his hero too. He also read works of pious biography: *The Flowers of the Saints*. He has told in his autobiography of how, as he lay powerlessly in bed, he was tortured by the desire for his old life as a lover and soldier, and how gradually—when he realized this was impossible—he decided to become the soldier of Christ, how the Virgin replaced in his mind the memory of his mistresses. When he was cured, he set off on his horse, giving out that he was going to rejoin his fellows in arms, but in fact privately deciding to go to the Benedictine monastery at Montserrat: not an exceptional decision in those times in Spain, for the army or the priesthood was the only acceptable vocation for men of condition.

On his journey across the mountains of Aragón to Montserrat, Loyola had his famous argument with the Moorish traveller. In the years of tolerance before the reconquest and the expulsion of the Jews, religious disputation had been common between the religionists and had even been formally organized, but the Moor added jokes to his arguments and made fun of the doctrine of the perpetual virginity of the Virgin Mary. Loyola was a soldier, but he was now on his way to becoming a mystical knight, and he was unable to decide whether or not to kill the Moor for the insult to his Lady. He left the decision to his mule. If the mule took the Moor's road when the two travellers parted, Loyola would kill the Moor. This prudent hesitation, this cautious looking for the guidance of the world or the pause in which other authority can direct the course, was prophetic of the Jesuit habit of mind and of the disturbing opportunism that appears side by side with the cult of obedience. The mule took the road to the Abbey. At Montserrat, Loyola made his knightly vigil in conscious imitation of Amadis.

Like Luther, like Santa Teresa, like all men in religious crises at that time, Loyola mortified his flesh. By fastings, which lasted a week, by daily scourgings.

The Spanish Temper

After his vigil at Montserrat he gave away his rich
clothes and dressed himself in some rough garment
and went limping to Manresa. This was a mountain
village and he lived in the House of the Poor. He
punished his vanity by neglecting his hair and letting
his nails and his beard grow. He begged in the streets.
By prayer, hunger, and self-torture he crushed the
memory of his sins. It was at Manresa, where twice he
nearly died of the suffering he inflicted upon himself,
that the famous, quixotic episode of the cave of
Manresa occurred—one can compare it with the experience of Don Quixote in Montesinos's cave—in
which he saw two knights of Good and Evil fighting
in armour for possession of his soul. At Manresa,
Loyola wrote his mystical work, the spiritual exercises.
They were written under the influence of a devout
lady of the place. Indeed, Loyola has been accused of
plagiarism. He wrote the rules "for overcoming oneself and for regulating one's life without being swayed
by any inordinate attachment." They aim at the destruction of the imagination and the will, the reduction
of the soul to the state of obedient automaton, but in
arriving at this result they take the student through
a terrible course of shamed self-knowledge and the
subtleties of scruple. They give him, if he survives, a
capacity and taste for power. Loyola is the great
schoolmaster soldier: like Lenin, the great Commissar

of his age. Blind obedience to the commander: that has always been the pole that magnetizes the anarchic Spaniard in his moments of energy; when that energy dies, then, *"se obedece, pero no se cumple"*—the casuistry begins.

Jesuitism is not a Spanish phenomenon; it is European. What is characteristically Spanish was its original military form and the doctrine of obedience to military orders. Many have noted the curious analogy of contemporary Communism: obedience was not possible until a revolution had taken place and Loyola had reformed the Papacy.

The Jesuits [says the Portuguese historian Martins in his *History of Iberian Civilization*] conceived and carried through the reform of the religion of the peoples of the South . . . by modifying the terrible doctrine of Grace, glossing over the rigid rules of the doctrine of the Church, and inventing a tolerant spiritual direction, a lax morality, an easy casuistry, a facile devotion, and the doctrine of probablism. They made a suitable and indulgent religion, and, to make it consistent, entrusted to a methodical and mechanical guidance of the imagination the part which in Protestantism belonged to the voice of conscience and an orderly existence. With the clear vision of genius, the Company discovered the true principle of educating men: to build up a sensuous atmosphere of the imagination which might give birth to ideas, suitably to preface the material in which to mould and fashion thoughts. Protestantism proceeded from the inside to the outside of man. Jesuitism reversed the process. The one was a republic, with the problems of its doctrines treated idealistically, the other was Cæsarism with all the practical problems of a religious state.

What is Spanish in Jesuitism is that short period of crisis and intensity in Loyola's life; and Jesuitism is so Italianate in its inspiration that, after Loyola's creative outburst, it has little connection with his life.

Chapter IV

Twenty-five years ago Madrid was a flat Spanish
city hardly visible on its cliff above the river
Manzanares except as a low line of heavy red roofs.
Only the large façade of the Royal Palace disclosed
the existence of a city as one approached it. Now
skyscrapers and tall white blocks of flats like up-
ended sugar cubes break the horizon and give the city
an American appearance from the distance. Large
white suburbs have sprung around it, and, like Barcelona, the capital has doubled its population in a
generation. Although it is despised by foreigners, who
find little of old Spain in it, for Madrid was built in

the seventeenth century at the orders of the King, it
is an agreeable modern city in the spring and the
autumn. Its harsh, wet or snowy, winter climate is
hard to bear, and the heat in July and August is intolerable. At this season all who can afford to do so
get out of the capital to the mountains or to the north;
those who stay resign themselves to very little sleep
because of the heat, and the population sits up half
the night in the streets.

The Talgo arrives at the right hour—the time of
the *paseo*, when the cafés are packed and the streets
are crowded with people in the sacred evening promenade of Spanish life. They have gone to the main
streets in the centre of the city, which has become a
hive. In some towns at this hour one is drawn by a
sustained, dry roar of voices which sounds like the
roar of a football match, a bullfight, or a political
meeting; but, making one's way towards it, through
streets that are strange because they are empty, one
arrives at the Plaza Mayor, or some street where the
traffic has been barred, to find most of the population
has gathered there by custom, to talk and walk end-
lessly round and round. The Spaniards have little social life in their houses—though a little social life imitated from Europe does go on among the better off or
the very Europeanized; tea parties and cocktail parties
are occasionally given by such people—the major-

ity of Spaniards treat the street as their place of entertainment.

At this hour the women appear and display themselves as if they had walked into a drawing-room. External display is important to Spaniards; they will spend more on their persons than on their houses, in which they easily dispense with the mania for furnishing and interior decoration which possesses northerners, and not entirely because the general standard of wealth is much lower. But in the street they dress well. Any Spanish crowd, even in the poor districts, is the best-dressed crowd in Europe, but they are rarely elegant or fashionable. They have simply a firm conservative sense of what is fitting, not of what attracts extravagant attention. Only in their jewelry do the Spanish women display extravagance.

There is no chic and there is no sophistication in Spain, not even in Madrid, except when it has obviously been imitated from Paris or brought in and Frenchified by South Americans; one is always struck by the conservative temperament of the people, their love of the purely formal, and even by a national provinciality. They have always kept to their own ways, have always sustained their own genre, and they withdraw, with a sort of disapproving or even positive scorn, from the contagion of other manners. In this they are resolute rather than complacent, egotistic rather than hostile—perhaps a little snobbish. In their preoccupation with what is "suitable" they resemble the English.

One finds a seat in a café and orders a glass of their iced beer and watches the crowd. One is deafened by their voices and the violent noise of the traffic. In England the general standard of looks is low; one is struck only by the large number of very individual faces which suggest that the English are characters out of Cruikshank's drawings. In France the standard of looks is not much higher than in England; at any rate in the north of France it is not. The Spaniard level is high; indeed, a certain regularity of feature, boldness of nose, and brilliance of eye appear to have been standardized. The amount of Jewish blood is, one would think, high. This is not as fantastic a generalization as it may sound: the Jewish population, open or hidden, was enormous in Spain, and the exodus cannot have excluded its deep racial infiltration altogether. There is a classical Spanish type, grave, dark, sallow, a little heavy sometimes; and there is the small, monkeyish type, quick, melancholy, mischievous. The crowd falls into those natural divisions which may be broken by an occasional woman of great beauty or a figure of grotesque ugliness. Only the old, bent, and ill carry themselves badly. Round shoulders are rarely seen. The dry, electric air of the city enlivens these walkers. One has the impression of great natural vitality, undistracted by northern nerves.

Many travellers have noticed what has seemed to them an almost racial difference between Spanish men and women. (The difference is really social: the life of the Spanish male is likely to be more anxious, less fulfilled than the life of the Spanish female. He is encumbered, as the woman is not exclusively, by the condition of Spain, the frustration of the will.) The women of Madrid, as they go by in their twos and threes, and so rarely with a man, have a militant, formal, prim appearance. Sociable and talkative—for all Spaniards love talking for its own sake—they are trained to a double role: they display themselves, they have great personal pride; yet never for one moment do they allow their eyes to meet the eyes of a man as they walk the street. The decorum is complete and is distinctly Victorian.

The Spanish language is decisive and quick, packed with turns of phrase. What is called *"gracia,"* a gay shrewdness in repartee rather than wit, is always sought. To a foreign ear, the language sounds granular and rapid, rather harsh and unmusical, and this gives a male assertiveness and roughness to the voices of the women. As they walk by, carrying themselves so well, they are rather a collected, rather severe female race.

The Spanish Temper

For all this dominant appearance—and they clearly dominate the men by having their role in life firmly marked out and mixed with the male role very little socially—they have the reputation of being homely, innocent, and sensual. They are passionate lovers of children: there is marriage and eight children in their eyes. Yet in the past ten or fifteen years Spain has gone through revolutionary changes, and Spanish girls are experiencing a belated and relative emancipation. One unexpected effect of the Civil War, although it ended with the victory of reactionary forces in religion and politics, is this emancipation of women. In the twenties and thirties, it is true that in educated families there was considerable freedom for women, especially for those who went to the Free or International schools. They could go about a good deal on their own, they took up intellectual careers, they travelled; most revolutionary, they read what they wanted and did not accept the censorship of the priests. (This is far from saying these girls were non-Catholics; they were deeply Catholic, but Spanish notions of what is suitable for girls to read are simple and severe. Spanish literature is barred to them—if they are obedient.) In the reaction that has followed under Franco, it is the fashion to despise the educated generation socially. It is not done to be educated; yet, paradoxically, the young girls now growing up have far more freedom of movement and go to university courses. Some cynical people think that this passion for socially despised education is a scheme for getting out of the house.

Display, a certain extravagance of state, is—by the continual paradox of Spanish life—loved by this frugal and sober people. The question has been gone into thoroughly by Galdós, the Spanish Balzac, as he is called, and moralist historian of the late nineteenth and early twentieth century. The moral basis of life in Madrid has been thoroughly described by this moralist who soaked himself in the life of all classes, and in spite of the social changes he is still a valuable guide. Societies do not change as fast as they like to think they do from generation to generation. Galdós went into the question of social state and display in his novel called *La de Bringas* and it is concerned with a family that spends everything on social position. In the golden age when the treasure was brought back from the Indies, in the time of Goya, when the *maja* and the *majo* wore their fantastic clothes, in the gorgeous uniforms of the various police forces which the Spaniard cannot do without, one can trace the phases of the Spanish extravagance.

In the past twenty-five years, and especially under the Franco regime, Madrid has gone in for architectural display. It now belongs to the exuberant group of southern cities, like Barcelona, Genoa, and Milan. The outburst has been stimulated by Fascist megalomania and bad taste, but it had started long before Franco. Like ambitious provincials, the Spaniards have gone in, architecturally, for the façade of modernity. Spain is a poor country which has been ruined by civil war and years of drought and famine. It has little industry, and in despair, after the Civil War, the peasants have left the land in tens of thousands to go into the cities. The population has enormously increased, which delights the chauvinists of the present regime, but the means of supporting this new huge population have not grown with it. (I saw this year a village in the south from which seven eighths of the population had gone, and the roofs of its empty houses had fallen in; and outside all the big towns are slums of temporary shacks, built of flattened tins. The government does all it can to stop this swarming in, and sends the Civil Guard to burn down these horrible places, but they soon spring up again.) Wages are very low, food is still very dear, the working population is living on a much lower standard than existed twenty years ago. The ordinary labourers' wages vary from twelve to seventeen pesetas a day and of this higher wage a car-park attendant said to me dryly: "It is a wage on which one cannot live, but one may die with dignity on it." The aim of General Franco's rebellion

89

was to crush the revolutionary movement which had risen during the slump of the thirties among the Spanish poor, and to meet their demands, after disbanding their political and trade-union organizations, by the "vertical corporations" on the Italian Fascist model. Economic conditions have been so bad, owing to war and drought, that one cannot tell whether this system works as a system or has been broken into a possible way of living by Spanish character. But these corporations are so organized that on no level can the worker have an independent, not to mention a decisive or powerful, voice. The position of some workers has improved where they were unorganized before —domestic servants are better off—and there are social services, like free medical attention and insurance, which did not exist before. Madrid is cynical about all this. Everyone delights in pointing out the fatal Spanish capacity for producing the perfect blueprint, which is never put into operation. Again—"We obey but we do not fulfil." The reform is not organic. It is imposed from above on the Spanish people. It is a form of display. Talk about it to any pragmatic Spanish workman. He answers in two dry sentences: "We are silenced. Look at my wages." If a foreigner asks the question, he soon finds himself the embarrassed centre of a protest meeting. And the law prohibits political discussions.

The Spanish Temper

The megalomaniac building has a bearing on this. It is the outlet of southern European regimes where the small middle class cannot face social problems. Certainly Franco has built workers' colonies and flats, rebuilt villages destroyed in the war, and, since the Spaniards are excellent domestic builders, these have been admirably done. Spanish bad taste comes out in public buildings, where there is money to burn. Just outside Madrid there is a suburb which has been called New Moscow and looks like it. The display-building of dictatorship is in the huge, ugly public monuments, the skyscrapers, the pretentious squares and blocks of government offices—these are nearly all unfinished, and no work has been done on them for years, so that they have not the merit of providing employment any more. The money has run out and one dare not consider how much of what is called "*El palacio que va d'espacio*"—the palace that goes slow —has gone down the drain of political and contractual rewards. The poorer classes regard these edifices with cynicism and bitterness.

As I have said, this architectural change has really been creeping on for a long time in Madrid. It began in what now (as one looks back upon it) must have been the peace and abundance of the first years of the century and in the time when Spain filled its pockets as a neutral in the First World War. Madrid first imitated Paris. Those dough-like balconies of the latest flats were copied from the Champ-de-Mars and Passy. The architectural beauty of Madrid lay in the seventeenth-century quarter, in the stately Plaza Mayor (now a semi-slum), in the beautiful, grave Ayuntamiento; after that in the sad, sedate, middle-class nineteenth-century air. The Spaniards had a certain grace in being out of date and behind the times. It was a sign of respectability, and this gave Madrid a firm Victorian charm which was in keeping with the easy, old-fashioned notions of its people. The chief cafés were comfortable and rather worn. The spittoon—the national grail of the period—was everywhere. One could walk down corridors of spittoons. The cafés were packed with men until three or four in the morning; respectable women did not often go to them, though here and there one might see a family. Even by the early thirties it was not common to see respectable women in cafés; foreign women were pitied for their social ignorance or "nervous" emancipation in going to them. In that old Madrid up to the thirties one was struck by the large number of priests in the middle of the city, huge amiable men in shabby hats, and smoking cigars as they strolled up and down—whereas now, no doubt because the Church is tactfully keeping their great number out of sight, there are very few. The cabinet minister used to walk with

his court of secretaries and sycophants, the most favoured walking next to the great man, who was commonly very fat. Spanish writers used to attack their
rulers for being so public and available and having no
regard for the reserves of office. The great generals
would have their court. They would sit in the cafés
with the courtesan of the moment. One would admire
the double chins of the rich or powerful and well-fed,
the remarkable bellies of the sad gluttons carrying
their burden before them with an air of martyrdom.

In this period Madrid produced—and it still produces—a large number of what can only be called
single-purpose men or Oblomovs. A number of these
might have the occupation of remaining in bed all
day and would rise at six merely to fulfil the function
of walking; others were devoted chiefly to sleep—I
remember a pleasant Marquis, a very intelligent man,
who must have been the æsthete of sleep, the Walter
Pater of the long torpid moment. Another I remember was a gambler, another a pursuer of women; many
were full-time talkers. Some sat alone. These were
their occupations, their entire life. In one Andalusian
town there was a man called "the night-husband," an
unhappy man who had two illegitimate families besides
his own—an Andalusian habit that is a throwback to
the harem system copied from the Moors—and who
was therefore known "to be unable to be about in the

daytime." Others were journalists who went to an office to talk, but who never wrote; many were contact men, who walked the streets in order to scrape acquaintance and hope for a commission to turn up. A large number of civil servants notoriously appeared at their offices only on pay day. These single-purpose men were not necessarily rich. They had some small rent, perhaps, and, having the Spanish instinct for frugal living and for finding the basic minimum of human need and effort, could live on that or perhaps on the subvention of an unprotesting relative. In every family there seemed to be one phenomenal man whose single function it unluckily was to work day and night, often at two or three different professions, so that he might be a solicitor for one part of the day, a civil servant at some other or an agent for a company, and in the evenings a journalist and a teacher. It was he who supported, without complaint, a large family of his own and a number of relations whose special gift happened to be the one of doing without regular employment. And even these workers had found a minimum: they had discovered quite naturally how to live on a minimum of pleasure.

Franco's victory has given a longer lease to the single-purpose man, and in countries where the middle class is relatively small, it is hard and aggressive in self-defence. Still the outward changes in twenty-four years are enormous. That preposterous South American street still called the Gran Vía, though it has been renamed Avenida José Antonio after Primo de Rivera's son, the Falangist leader who was shot in one of the earliest vengeances of the Civil War, has been extended and completed. Instead of the old Victorian cafés, new marbled bars of luxury and pretence have been built. The famous jam of yellow trams, moving at a quarter of a mile an hour and stuck fast between the Puerta del Sol and the Post Office, has gone. The trams are blue, the traffic moves fast. The super-cinema has arrived, with its huge melodramatic posters; the radios bawl out their *flamenco* songs; in the hot weather the canned voices from the screen of the open-air cinemas can be heard shouting two or three streets away, and since the cinemas go on till nearly two in the morning, no one who lives near can sleep.

Intellectual life is certainly in eclipse—and literary society is so alive with malicious rumour and scandal that one cannot do more than crudely suggest the obvious reasons: political and ecclesiastical censorship. The former is not considered as harmful as one would suppose, because Spain is politically tired out; the clerical censorship is another matter. It is intensely disliked, for it is as gross as the censorship in Eire. Writers have told me that the text of the classics and of recent writers like Galdós and Valle-Inclán has been tampered with. I do not know whether this is so, but it is hard to get necessary books in Spain. I know that the foreign interest in Galdós has taken booksellers by surprise: French tourists and students cleared his works from the bookshops in Barcelona. A young Spanish novelist—who was unable to publish his last book in Spain and lost his job in the Censor's office—a favourite bread-and-butter occupation for writers—defined the intellectual's case by raising his glass "To the Pope's intentions."

In one sense, the present intellectual sterility in Spain is due to the swing of the pendulum. Between 1898 and the 1930's, Spanish literature was written by a brilliant school of inquirers and pessimists, two of whom—Unamuno and Ortega y Gasset—came to have European reputations. In education there were Giner de los Ríos, and Cossío, the authority on Greco; in science Cajal; in music Falla; in poetry the Machados and Lorca. Benavente, the dramatist, won the Nobel Prize; Baroja, Ayala, and several others were very good novelists. There was Azorín, the exquisite and learned essayist. To these must be added the political writers Araquistain, who became Communist, Maeztu—who was executed—who became Fascist. In the twenties and thirties there was intellectual excitement in Madrid, and Spanish history might have turned out differently if Primo de Rivera (a benevolent and practical despot) had been able to obtain the support of the intellectual movement. He could not, because he was in the hands of the two forces the intellectuals always opposed: the Army and the Church. The renaissance simply exhausted itself. Its leaders are old or dead or in exile.

A very large number of the best liberal or independent minds were driven for a long time and even permanently out of Spain by the Civil War. The educated classes left because they hated the two main factions. General Franco has now left it open for his opponents to return without molestation, and some have done so; but most of them remain in France, England, and South America. These exiles are often embittered, for they have seen the work of a whole generation of educators, reformers, men of science, and artists destroyed first, and superseded. And, as always happens when exile is long enough, the Spanish exiles are either out of touch or they have struck roots elsewhere. Most of them are intellectuals, and are not rich; how would they live if they returned? Another party or another generation has stepped into their shoes. In politics, the exiled not only are out of touch with what is really going on inside Spain, but are incurably divided among themselves, quarrelling over a major cause of their defeat: the intolerance and fanatical quarrels of the Left-wing sects. In politics the exiles, generally, are more extreme than people of the same complexion in Spain and are dated. These wish to forget the Civil War and its appalling personal losses; the business of surviving the terrible time after the Civil War, of keeping their heads above water, of getting enough to eat, has bewildered and exhausted them, whereas the exiles are fixed in the past. Beyond the frontier is Spanish pride, inside the frontier is Spanish compliance and the dread of going through it all again. Scepticism has come in:

"I see no difference between Franco and Communism," says the Left-wing hotel proprietor—nothing more absurd than to imagine the Left or "Reds" consisted only of the poor and propertyless.

"I was jailed by Franco," said a publisher, "and I hate the present regime, yet perhaps, after all, things have turned out better than we thought they would."

"After Franco?"

"We have shown ourselves to be barbarians, fanatics, and extremists: we must dread the future."

All they know is that the Civil War was a revolution that has made a complete break between the generations.

The Gran Vía and the Castellana (the wide avenue which runs from the ugly Post Office to the outskirts of the city, where the road to France begins) are lined with soldiers in khaki and German-style steel helmets. They look as though they had slept all night in their rumpled uniforms, which were made in the cheap factories of Catalonia, and they stand slack, sunburned, apathetic, and with a kind of homely individual rebelliousness, the very opposite of a military machine.

"What a lot! The poor mugs," mocks the taxi-driver, a man of an older generation, as one drives by. "Standing there like sticks. Do this! Do that! Doing what the officers tell them. We never took any notice of any officers in my time." He goes on shouting with laughter all down the line as we drive by and ends up with some old soldier story about hiding a platoon in the cook-house. All this is the usual ridicule of Madrid, the old Sancho Panza coming out, the old hatred of discipline; all the same, the spirit of working-class Madrid is deeply anti-Franco. In the good regiments there is a better turn-out than this, in imitation of the Germans, but generally the Spanish Army looks baffled, hopeful rather than efficient. These soldiers must be very different from the former highly trained Spanish infantry of the time of Charles V, but we remember that the Republican Spaniards made short work of the Italians in the Civil War, which indicates what they can do when they are well led.

Since the Napoleonic Wars the Spaniards have become a nation of guerrilla fighters—they invented the word for this kind of fighting—and perhaps in this they reverted to the traditional methods of warfare which they had employed in the reconquest of Spain from the Moors. The fighting in the Civil War was sharp—though the casualties in the field were far lower than the loss of life by civilian massacre, execution, and murder—and when we consider that one side (the Franco side) had the enormous advantage of war material from Germany and Italy, the length of the war indicates the stubbornness of Spanish fighting even when it was ill-matched. It is true that the Republican side was stiffened by foreign battalions and Russian advisers and that the war was also prolonged by the incurable quarrels on the Republican side and the incompetence on the side of Franco; but the unyielding quality of the fighting is obvious in all accounts.

The taxi-driver belonged to the old Spanish Army, the poor, ill-fed, ill-armed hungry lot who were not so healthy-looking as these men are. He was not old enough to have belonged to the generation which had known the catastrophe of Annual in Morocco, when a whole army was wiped out in 1921 by the Moors of Abd el Krim. The Spanish commanding officer committed suicide in the field in that disaster, which was caused by the grossest corruption in the higher ranks of the Army. (Up to the time of the Republic there were nine hundred generals.) Alfonso XIII had been the driving force behind the Moroccan campaign, and he had always relied upon the Army because it was more stable than the civilian parties; he managed to stave off the consequences of Annual by putting in Primo de Rivera as a dictator, but by 1931 civilian Spain had had enough, and the King wisely went.

The troops line the Castellana and the Gran Vía because General Franco is driving by. One sees the amiable little fat man standing up in his car, trim, dignified, and homely. The crowd is pretty considerable. It loves to see his Moorish bodyguard, though there must be many who have other feelings about the Moors, especially in Madrid. The people are waving to the only surviving Fascist dictator in western Europe, the one friend and ally of Hitler and Mussolini to survive in a world utterly hostile to him. He is the ghost of that old guilty fear of Hitler and Mussolini which paralysed French, English, American, and Russian politics in the thirties, for without the help of arms and technicians and men from the Axis powers Franco would not have won the Civil War. Indeed, after the first set-back before Madrid (indeed, long before that, when it was obvious that Spain was divided in two) he would have been the usual Spanish general who makes a *coup d'état* and fails. There would have been no mass massacres, no secret and murderous tribunals, no famine and destruction. Would there have been a Red revolution, as the propaganda of General Franco has always asserted? Who can tell? A counter *coup d'état* by a "liberal" general seems just as likely; the material aid of the Russians was small compared with what was at once received by the servant of Mussolini and Hitler—the bombing of Guernica, the bombardment of the refugees from Málaga to Almería, were German military exercises.

Franco was allowed to succeed because the French, English, and Americans were afraid of Hitler and Mussolini; he survives because of the fear of aggression from Russia. Franco's argument is that he is the last line of defence against Russian Communism if it attacks. He trades, politically and financially, on that fear. He also relies on the fact that no two Spaniards, in exile or in the country, can agree on what should succeed him. Foreigners burn their fingers in Spanish affairs, which pride and the fragmentation of politics make exasperating and dangerous. In the ordinary course of European life what happens in Spain is of negligible importance; in two world wars the neutrality of Spain has been desired by all, for even Hitler blew hot and cold on the subject of Spanish intervention. The dangerous aspect of American aid to Spain is that it extends the possible war area and makes

The Spanish Temper

Spanish neutrality impossible. Like Russia, Spain was a disaster to Napoleon; its population, quiet at first, soon rises spontaneously and furiously against any occupying army and aggravates any conqueror without providing advantage or reward. The Spaniards are blest with an exorbitant sense of what they can demand for doing next to nothing; this satisfies their pride and enables the negotiator to withdraw with indignation. It was General Franco's policy—as it had been Alfonso XIII's in 1914—to be practical and realistic, to get valuable pickings from both sides and to keep out of Europe. On the whole we may be glad of Spanish realism; whether all Spaniards can rejoice in it is another matter.

Franco's meeting with Hitler at Hendaye in October 1940 was one of the comical incidents of the war. It was a meeting between northern romance, gesture, and vagueness with Spanish evasiveness and precision. After it Hitler said that, rather than go through another interview with Franco, he would sooner have three or four teeth out. Hitler came for his reward for having supported General Franco in the Civil War; the General asked for large pieces of French Africa, Gibraltar, and also for food and oil. The last was the vital thing for a Spain that was broken and starving; Hitler could not supply them and not even the bait of capturing Gibraltar would tempt the General. When it comes down to a question of necessity, the Spaniards do not really want Gibraltar; they want its nuisance value. The Allies kept Franco quiet by small allowances of food and oil—see an excellent article by Hugh Trevor-Roper in the *Observer* of June 7, 1953—put up with Franco's pin-pricks until the tide of war turned.

Within Spain the conservatives and the Right have usually been pro-German. The choice is instinctive in authoritarians. I once watched a German director training singers in a Spanish choral society, years before the war; they behaved slackly or extravagantly as Spanish artists often do; the German became hysterical, savage and relentless in his drilling, forcing them to do what he wanted. The ordinary French, Italian, or English director would have relied on willingness, persuasion, slow education, on those techniques which are natural to free people, and in doing so would either have made little progress or have allowed the singers to drift into those bad habits the Spaniards so readily pick up from foreigners. The German allowed no freedom. He drilled violently. The Spaniards became themselves. They appear to thrive on authority.

The liberals or Left in Spain have generally been Anglophile by a tradition that runs through the nineteenth century and which was fostered by English commercial power. When Britain reversed the old

policy of backing the Left against the Right in the
1930's, it strengthened the hostile and reactionary
forces in Spain and got little but contempt and insult
for doing so. The friends of Britain in Spain are, however, still the same: most of the intellectual classes and
the Left wing. They worked, often at personal risk,
to help the Allies in the war; and they know that if the
cold war is closed, the period of reaction in Spain will
come to an end.

General Franco is the conventional soldier-dictator
of the type that has appeared regularly in Spanish life
since the Napoleonic Wars. He differs considerably
from his predecessor of the twenties, Primo de Rivera,
who was a liberal-minded Andalusian and no great
Catholic. General Franco is without brilliance; he is a
routine officer, simple, pious, and—very unusual in
Spanish politics—of blameless private life. Primo de
Rivera reluctantly gave in to the pressure of the militant Church; General Franco eagerly does so. He
keeps his position by playing off the three forces of
contemporary Spanish politics—the Church, the
Army, and the Falange—against each other. The
Falange began as a crusade, turned into a lower-mid-
dle-class Fascist movement which drew its member-
ship from Communist and Anarcho-syndicalist groups;
it is fundamentally anticlerical. The intolerance which
followed on its triumph in the war has been worn

down by fourteen years of power, by rewards in the form of titles, offices, contracts. Its syndicalist theory accords with Spanish social temperament; it runs schools and youth organizations and bedevils Spanish life. The greatest circumspection has to be shown by professional men, or they may find their means of livelihood gone. I have never heard the Falange taken seriously as a force of social reform, and certainly its drastic political power has declined; but it continues to have great power of annoyance in the press, and its main evil has been intellectual. If one compares the Spanish press of the twenties and thirties with the press of today, the loss is enormous.

There are really only three permanent forces in Spanish politics: the Church, the Army, and the people. The last are incalculable. They remain for long periods resigned, docile, quiet, and fatalistic. They are absorbed only in the affairs of their locality. But on certain occasions they have risen ferociously and spontaneously against those who are governing them. They rise, it must be said, in a primitive way, and have been generally hostile to Europeanism and outside influences. Their rebellion against the French on the Dos de Mayo in the Napoleonic Wars is famous: they rose then not only against the foreigner, but against the ideas of the Revolution. They rose in Catalonia against the Moroccan War. They rose in 1936 against

The Spanish Temper

General Franco himself when he landed in Spain from Morocco and brought Moors and Italians to fight his own people. They turned upon the Russian advisers on the Republican side.

It cannot be assumed that the Spanish people who rose then were similar to the progressive, revolutionary proletarians who make up the Left-wing parties in Europe. As so many foreigners discovered to their cost, the Left in Spain had a merely superficial and rhetorical identity with the views of communists, socialists, liberals, or anarchists (if they existed) outside of Spain. The Spanish masses are not an industrial proletariat, and even when they are peasants, they are so many different kinds of peasant that there is no natural unity of interest between them. At the time of the Republic, the Left was unable to decide whether it would aim at an agriculture of small peasant proprietors or one of large collectives; and the peasants themselves reject the notion of revolutionary progress, which to them is tainted by the evils of modern life. They look back to a golden age. In a large part of Extremadura many years ago I remember talking to anarchist railway men who (at that time) had joined the anarchists in order that they would not have to strike, because "all men should be brothers." They were quite willing to shoot down the employers and the socialist workers, on the ground that these groups were partners in the same wicked modern system. The socialists themselves were hampered by the "materialism" of the European and American workers. There *is* a liberal Spain, and a very strong one, which in every generation carries on a difficult campaign against the reactionary forces who have the power, but the liberals are generally middle-class individuals or small groups who have some notion of life over the frontier; and both the mass of the people and the rulers oppose them. These liberals themselves do not believe in "progress" as a vague general faith or hope, in our fashion. They concern themselves with particular unnecessary evils: the huge illiteracy and lack of schools, for example, the fundamental freedoms which are lacking, the serfdom of the south. They are far from wishing to introduce the freedom to have washing machines, television sets, motor-cars for all. With the possible—and doubtful—exception of industrial Catalonia, no one wants this; and indeed, when one has considered all the bitter miseries of Spanish life, all the barbarous injustices, all the wretchedness which comes from corrupt government, and when one wonders how it is that nevertheless great personal freedom exists there in a people who live with little feeling of social responsibility to one another, the only conclusion is that they are exclusively concerned with the primitive needs of man. The "wants" are despised. Even those who make money or are well off do not kill themselves to make more; there is far more regard for fortune than for the tedious rewards of industry. Hogarth's industrious apprentice or the trite figure of the ingenious Robinson Crusoe knocking up a bungalow on a desert island are unknown to the Spanish imagination. Money or fortune—those alone are acceptable; and bribery and corruption and "influence" are considered to be more humane than the pious accountancy of the just return.

The reactionary aspect of Left-wing politics was shrewdly noted by Franz Borkenau during the Civil War, and his words are worth reading now because they are still true. In *The Spanish Cockpit* he points out that there is a vast difference between the conscious and unconscious utterances made by Spaniards on behalf of the Spanish people, and that the unconscious is always protesting against Europe and the foreigner:

In the upper stratum: decay, corruption, political incapacity, as well as complete lack of creative power in any other respect. Below: fanaticism, capacity for self-sacrifice, spontaneity of action, but of action in a narrow, local, prejudiced sense without constructive capacities on a wider scale. Such was the structure of Spain at the beginning of the nineteenth century and such it has remained to this day. The content of the political antagonism has changed, but the cleavage between the two strata has remained and broadened. It is the distinguishing feature of Spain as compared with other countries who regard themselves as more progressive.

In other countries, every popular movement originated in the higher stratum of society; in modern Spain, no movement in the higher classes ever penetrated the masses:

In Spain the masses revolted, and, basically, still revolt against all sorts of progress and Europeanization, and, at the same time, take the lead in more than one great historical crisis, of the nation as a whole. . . . The Spanish masses hated and hate this modern civilization which is forced upon them.

Yet the hatred of European modern civilization is true of the Spanish upper stratum as well. There is always in Spanish life this attraction to Europe, but there is a permanent reaction from it. The Spanish intellectuals who from 1898 onwards preached Europe continually, always hedged a little. Large numbers of Spanish anticlericals always insisted that they were not anti-Catholic; or if anti-Catholic, not irreligious in the manner of the corresponding groups in France or Italy. The word "conscience" continually crops up in Spanish disputes and, in a pragmatic way, it connotes something of the lawyer's and casuist's keenness in the fine issue and, on a higher plane, something like a personal mysticism.

The Spanish Temper

The violence which has regularly broken out in Spain since the Napoleonic Wars is the reaction of a primitive people to the seeping in of industrial civilization. So much of Spanish life is locked up or emotionally fixed in the spirit of the Middle Ages—Unamuno said: "I feel within myself a mediæval soul"—that the adjustment to industrial civilization is an agony. Spain hated and rejected the Reformation, the Renaissance, and the French Revolution.

It is typical of Spain that when the split between Marx and Bakunin occurred in the nineteenth century, the Spanish revolutionaries preferred the decentralized freedom of the Russian anarchist to the central tyranny proffered by the German Jew. The strength of anarchism before the Civil War in Spain was phenomenal, and the movement was unique in Europe. Even now, when anarchism has been driven underground—for it can hardly be crushed; its very defeats confirm it in its hatred of contemporary governments —it is still the only body which sends its agents over the Pyrenees to maintain the underground movement. Anarchism took strong root in Spain partly because it is a country of isolated towns and villages, each capable of a self-contained life on its own; and partly because it meant the total rejection of industrial civilization in its middle-class or socialistic form. No political totalitarianism! The only totalitarianism the anarchists

can admit—and their theory obviously implies it—
is spiritual or theocratic. Anarchism was religious, and
Catholic absolutism had, by an irony, prepared the
ground for it. Once the land was taken from the
Church in the nineteenth century, once the mediæval
system was broken up and the Church lost its contact
with the people, a large number of the peasants sought
for a millennial faith elsewhere; the burnings and mur-
ders of anarchism must be compared with the *auto de
fe* of the Absolute Church, with the desire to preserve
purity. The link of the most idealistic anarchists with
gunmen and criminals has a sort of poetic logic: Robin
Hood and the bandit are the products of agrarian war.

The history of the Republic from 1931 to 1939 has
disillusioned Spaniards about themselves. The early
achievements of the Republic were important, but
savage intolerance soon swept them away. It was mad
to open an all-out attack on the Catholic Church, it
was mad to potter with the land question; but each
section of the Right and Left wanted its own absolute,
without compromise and without even some small
show of practical sense. Each party fell into the hands
of its own extremists.

Now Spain is exhausted and cynical and silenced
by guilt about the Civil War. They do not care much
to talk about it, and, indeed, it is a long time ago.

Industrialism and modern life come in, a quiet process of Europeanization goes fitfully on: the factories go up, the roads are built, the dams are constructed, the movement to study abroad—begun in the early years of this century—has not been stopped. The Civil War itself was a revolution which got out of the hands of the victors and the losers, for the village pattern was broken up by massacre, exile, travel, the flight to the big towns. In industrial regions, like Catalonia, a younger generation regards the ageing heroes of the Civil War with respect, but also with wonder and amusement. This young generation accepts the break with custom and traditions eagerly.

In the meantime chauvinists and the Falange are exuberant about the huge increase in population. When one asks how a poor country like Spain is to support such a population, they answer that industrialism will support it. They talk of new hydroelectric plants and factories. They talk of tractors—which would destroy the soil of Castile in a single summer. They ignore the new slums, which recall to the English reader the terrible history of the English industrial cities when the peasantry swarmed into the towns. Certainly in the big Spanish cities there is a façade of luxury; there is a fantastic luxury for the rich; there is a vulgar luxury for the small middle class, at any rate for the young of that class on whom the burdens of Spanish life have not yet fallen. The popular night clubs and cinemas have a cheap popular luxury. But millions of Spaniards in town and country live far below the level of these pleasures.

As one watches the General drive by, one sees the head of a state which is trading on its chance of surviving on American money. Since a great deal of foreign money is pouring into Spain from tourism—which is admirably organized—and because of America's strategic interest in Spain, the appearance of prosperity increases. It is a picture which could, no doubt, be matched in most European countries since the war—but what happens when the war-scare goes, and when we no longer live on the mysterious capital of our strategic importance?

Chapter V

In Italy we are all the time aware of our civilization and of the substance and lineament it has inherited from Greece and Rome. We are conscious of the heroic pagan world in Sicily and everywhere of Greek and Roman art and the pagan sun. Not so in Spain, except a little on its eastern, Mediterranean coast. There is something, of course, to remind us of a pre-Christian world. We can begin with the cave drawings of Altamira; we can see the beautiful Greek Lady of Elche in the Prado, which still stores the Mediterranean honey in its stone; we can see the mine shafts of the Carthaginians in Murcia. At Mérida, there is a very great deal of Rome; at Toledo the Roman bridge; and in the east are the Roman triumphal arches that stand, still golden, and where the bees hum in the ilex on the Valencia road, and in the enormous walls of the castles there. But no temples, no populations of statuary; even when the Renaissance comes to Spain it is sedate.

The Spaniards are patently Christian soldiers and Christian totalitarians. They built for fortification, for the display of state and power, for use and the prestige of families. In all towns one finds the massive, plain wall, with the noble gate and the extravagant scutcheon over it. In the works of art, the impression is of how important were the dead of the town, now redeemed by the blood of Christ, the intercession of the only true Church. Spain is a country of great shrines and great tombs. We think of the shrines of Covadonga and Montserrat—alas, now branches of the religious tourist industry—of St. James at Compostela and of the Virgin of the Pilar in Zaragoza; of seminaries like those of Salamanca and Comillas; of monasteries like the Escorial, Guadalupe, and half-ruined Poblet in the Catalonian mountains, of the Charterhouse that stands outside Burgos on the edge of the dunes; of innumerable smaller religious houses with their hard, dead, bucketing bells; gravity, power, and reserve from without, ease and fantasy within. Their high and massive dusty walls are not to be argued with; within are their carved cloisters and colonnades, the useful refectories, the sombre, gold-laden or sugary chapels, and those sweet, watered gardens with their flowers and their cool, timeless silence, shut away from the dust, the wind, the raucous extremity of Spanish life. How simply, frugally, nobly, how decorously and with what simple family graciousness the Spaniards have lived in these walls amid the harsh life of their country! One travels from sumptuous tomb to tomb; from one heavily populated altar with its huge progeny of saints, prophets, and apostles to the next. The clever Italians find this sombre, monotonous, and anti-human: what a narrow passion for immortality the dramatic Spaniard had! How easily he shut himself up within his own skin or within monastic or cathedral walls, in conventional and passive contemplation! The monastic population was once immense in Spain, as one can see from the history of Guadalupe or in the massive fortified ruins of Poblet. This was the richest monastery in Europe, favoured by kings. It was pillaged by the Napoleonic French, who stripped Spain of as much art as they could carry away. Poblet was less a monastery than an immense agricultural estate, the mill and granary of a region; landlord, market, and borough in itself. Under the impulse of the present Catholic drive in Spain great sums are being spent on

Poblet, and the Spaniards are excellent and scholarly restorers. A small religious order lives there, and one peeps through the small glass window into the modern dining-hall of the order. Decently done in the light polished oak, it suggests the modern college or hostel, the seat of a solemn summer school. One realizes how rich and how tenaciously interrelated the modern Catholic bureaucracy is.

I talked about the destruction of Poblet to the custodian there. At one moment he was saying how rich Poblet used to be, and the next, referring to the attacks on the priests and the burning of churches in the Civil War, he sighed piously and said:

"What wrong have the priests done, these good men? The mob, in its blindness, always attacks the innocent."

Innocence is a word one could certainly use to describe the humbler priesthood; but it is not a word one can apply to the Party—whether it is ripe and mediæval or raw and modern. The authority of the Church in Spain has passed out of the spiritual life into the social, political, and temporal. There one meets the packed committee, the Party nominees, the infiltrations of the members of Opus Dei who work, exactly in Communist fashion, to frustrate professional groups. It is impossible for a foreigner to state or judge the extent of the struggle: the liberty of the press has gone, and it is as impossible to publish an anti-clerical view, or one hostile to the view of the Church on any matter in Spain, as it would be to advocate private capitalism or non-official views in Russia.

One is bound to digress, in this fashion, when one is looking at Spanish architecture and art, for at its highest it is ideological and restrictive. How restrictive, how violently anti-humanist, one can say when one compares any example of it with the supreme genius of the Italians. Yet when one looks at Spanish painting and sculpture by the great masters, one is moved by an intense and individual quality, some strong and native strain which will not be found elsewhere. It is a quality of mind and temperament; a large part of it can be called dramatic psychological realism. I have known hundreds of Spaniards in all classes, and it has never seemed to me that they were, on the whole, very imaginative people, for their powerful egotism has been of the kind that cannot put itself in another creature's place or transcend its own personality. One is told, by Spanish writers, that Spaniards day-dream very little. Race and climate have, however, turned them into brilliant intellectual observers, more penetrating than affective or sympathetic. No aspect of real life repels or shakes them. They are subtle psychologists, though not to the point of speculation. Above all, they see the mind in the body, and the spiritual world is the physical world for them: the sanctity of the saint is to be seen in his literal wounds, his sick body. To Santa Teresa the soul is a garden. The love of the soul for the divine spouse is indistinguishable, in its phases, from earthly desire; because of the process of transference, her apprehension of love is sharper and more exact. French writers have also been superb psychologists but, in their case, they have worked within the abstract frame of a general idea: hatred is this, avarice is the other, love and anger are yet other intellectual concepts. Such intellectual concepts are lacking in the Spaniards, who look to a personal statement first. There is no ideal love, there is no abstract love; if they lay down an absolute towards which we toil, it will be in human terms—the love of the divine spouse, the love of the Virgin. And so, as psychologists, they excel in the photographic portraiture of psychological action. For them, in other words, any state of the soul is a state of *observable* drama. Spanish realism is bold, minute, unafraid, carnal, and limited to itself.

In the mornings in Madrid we used to go to the Prado. The slow walk was like a swim through the sunlight, and it was a preparation for the intense life we should see there. The Spanish streets prepare one for the unabashed records of Spanish painting—a dwarf, an idiot, a deaf and dumb couple laughing, a pair of blind lovers, a beggar or two have their picaresque place in the unpreoccupied crowds. We used to go, for a moment and mainly to get out of the heat for a minute or two, into any church on our way, and we used to notice the difference of worship between Spanish and Italian custom. For whereas in Italy the churches were places for wandering in and camping in, places used by life, which continually flowed into them from outside, and God's familiar market places, the Spanish churches were used by people with a strong sense of purpose and *tenue*. It was on our way to the Prado that I saw an old man kneeling before the crucified Christ in one of the Jesuit churches, a figure splashed by blood specks and with raw wounds, gaping as they would upon the mortuary slab, the face torn by physical pain, the muscles and tendons stretched. One imagined that the sculptor must have copied a crucified model to be so inflexible an anatomist and that the thought of *imagining* the agony of Christ had been beyond him. Before this figure kneeled an old man, and tears ran down his cheeks like the real-seeming tears glazed on the cheeks of the Christ; and, as he prayed, the old man kissed and caressed the toes, the calves, the knees of the figure and held them also with his hands. What grief, what dread or longing the old man was thus transposing one could not know, but one saw how his prayer depended utterly upon the communication of the senses, that he worshipped carnally and conceived of his acquaintance with God as a physical thing. If he described his God, the description would be physical, and the nature of his God would be a minute copy of his own or, if not a copy, a detailed response in the man's own terms.

I am not an art critic, but since I live chiefly by the eye, I get more pleasure out of painting and sculpture than any other arts. I have a purely literary point of view; that is to say, when I see a picture I find myself turning it into writing about human nature, habits of mind, the delight of the senses—all that is meant to me by "the pride of life." As one looks at the paintings of the Spanish, sombre as so many of them are whether they are earthly or religious, one sees what a great volume of emotion these minutely watched figures contain. How closely the great Spanish painters watch, sometimes for every detail, always for the key dramatic detail, the clue to a character, the spring of action! The faces and the bodies are caught at the moment of movement from one state of mind or feeling to another. The painters are not copyists from a still model; they are readers of nature; their view of nature might be described as the view of creative criticism. At the first acquaintance, with Velásquez's portraits of the court of Philip IV, even with that enchanting picture of the naughty Princess, *Las Meninas*, or with the picture of those arrogant and stubborn dwarfs, one sees the infinitely patient copyist who never conveys more than the visual scene before him; but presently we observe he is a painter of light, a critic of reflections. We see that he has caught the trance of human watchfulness, as if he had caught a few hard grains of time itself. Life is something pinned down by light and time. He has frozen a moment, yet we shall feel that it is a moment at its extreme point; that is, on the point of becoming another moment. If he is the most minute observer in the world, notice how his subjects are caught, themselves also minutely watching the world, with all the concentration the hard human ego is capable of. This is what living is to the human animal: it is to look. To look is to be. We see in Velásquez, as in all the Spaniards, the marriage of mind and eye. No painting could be, in the northern sense, less suggestive of a life without other accoutrement than the body and the habit of the hour.

The sensibility, the pride, the sensuous weakness of the court of Philip IV, where the decadence put out its first flowers in Spanish life, before the fruit formed and rotted, are seen in the realism of Velásquez. In an earlier painter like Zurbarán, in Greco, even in Murillo, and finally in Goya, the same basic, psychological

123

dramatic realism can be seen. We cannot doubt that thus life was, was seen and felt to be. And it is part of the genius of such exact penetration to horrify us with the tacit questions: What for? To what end? Behind such certainty is the certainty of death. The mad pride of the Duchess of Alba, her eccentric vanity! The homely foolishness of Charles IV, the total crookedness of Fernando VII! Goya caught the lowness of his world, its surrender of all style, its survival by a sort of ape-like impudence and by the shamelessness of Spanish vitality. The court did not object to these blistering portraits, but having no idea of themselves and no idea by which they lived, were grossly contented with the sight of their own likenesses.

Goya's savage anticlerical pictures are not now shown in the Prado, but they are well known. The satire of Goya is savage, but this distortion—like the very different distortions of El Greco—does not lessen his realism. This realism in Spaniards proceeds out of hot blood, not coolness. When Goya draws scenes of war, he feels the madness of action, its giddy and swooning movement, the natural boiling up of all human feeling towards crisis and excess, and it is in this state of mind that his eye becomes receptive to detail. Once again: psychological realism is not psychological analysis or speculation after the event, but the observation of the event in the tremor and heat of occurrence.

The Spanish Temper

Goya does not draw torture, rape, murder, hangings, the sadism of guerrilla warfare rhetorically, patriotically, or with a desire to teach, but he is as savage in his realism or his satire as the war itself. He is identified with it, and eventually he was driven out of his mind by acts which he could not forget. The nightmares themselves are horrible in their animality.

The terrifying quality of Goya's *Disasters of the War* springs, in part, from the comeliness and vanity of the human victims, from their complacency. There are no standard figures, but a great gallery of diverse characters whose ruling passion is clear in their faces. Each one palpably lives in his senses and, in the moment of death, their horrified eyes see the loss of the body. Goya's realism marries fury, insanity, corruption, whatever the state or passion is, to the body; it gives body to the sadism, the venom, the thieving, the filthy-mindedness, the smugness, the appalled pity of massacre.

Goya lived in a revolutionary age and turned from the traditional obsessions of the Spanish, with their religion and their lordliness, to the life of the populace of Madrid. There were three cults of the people in his time; some members of the upper classes took pleasure in following popular fashions in dress and put on the exaggerated, bold finery of the dandy or *majo*. The Duchess of Alba's picture in the Prado shows her in the costume of the *maja*—the full yellow dress, the black mantilla. There was a taste for fantasy and vulgarity in behaviour, ornament and exhibitionism in speech. The celebrated Spanish oath *Caramba* is taken from the stage name of a singer of *tonadilla* or one-act comic opera popular at the time. Goya drew her portrait, too. Goya's picture of the royal family represents them as ordinary people without kingliness or pride. Maria Luisa looks like a washerwoman, Fernando like a lackey. The cult of the people also had its political aspect and derived from the welcome given by the liberal-minded to the ideas of the French Revolution, but here "the People" is one of those alien political abstractions which Spaniards always, in the end, reject. The Spanish populace rose in Goya's time—but against the Revolution and the invader. The emotion was primitive, chauvinist, and patriotic. It was spontaneous, brave, and wild. The men who are being shot down in Goya's *Dos de Mayo* are ordinary Spaniards off the street.

This popular spirit has always existed in Spain; it is the bottomless well of Spanish vitality and exuberance, so that where there is deadness and corruption in the higher levels of society, there is always this creative energy underneath. It shows itself in the vitality of the popular arts. The Spaniards have a genius for popular display: the bullfight, the religious procession, and the fiesta. They have a genius for dancing and for the popular song. In the past thirty years there has been a slight decline in the typical regional character of this popular culture, but it remains easily the strongest and most lively in Europe. Even the decline, which is due to industrialism and better communications from one region to another, is less dangerous than it might seem. Spanish vitality is so great that it can digest the most awkward extraneous elements. The Spaniards have a genius for adapting everything to their own life; their indolence, the obstinate, individual refusal to break easily with custom, has given them enormous, natural power of resistance.

The radio blares from every street corner, but it is not often blaring the last American songs and dance tunes. Almost always the tune is *flamenco*, or *cante hondo*, a song from a popular *zarzuela* or musical comedy, a Spanish march. Once one is across the frontier, one is aware of being outside of Europe musically. One hears a new cadence, haunting, monotonous, yet also of pronounced dramatic rhythm. It is the rhetoric of music, sometimes tragic and grave, sometimes swanking and feverish with a swirl of skirts in it, sometimes Oriental and gypsy-like, lyrical and sad. The ear catches the strange notes of the cadence at once—la, sol, fa, mi—in the singing voice or in the guitar.

After midnight in Madrid, when one has just finished dinner one goes off into those packed, narrow streets lying off the Puerta del Sol in the middle of the city. They are streets of small bars crowded with men roaring away at each other, drinking their small glasses of beer or wine, tearing shellfish to bits and scattering their refuse and the sugar-papers of their coffee on the floors. The walls are tiled and in gaudy colours. The head of a bull will hang there, or some bloody painting of a scene at the bullfight. Through the door at the back of the bar one makes one's way into a private room, tiled again, like a bathhouse, and furnished only with a table and a dozen chairs. There one can invite a guitarist and singers and listen to *cante flamenco*.

Less respectably, one can find some cellar in the same quarter, some thieves' kitchen which will probably be closed by the police in a week or two, and there one may hear *cante flamenco* and, even better, the true *cante hondo*, or deep song, brought up in the last thirty years from the south, and sung not for the traveller's special entertainment but, as it were, privately, for the singer's own consolation. For, despite its howling, it is also an intimate music, perhaps for a singer and a couple of friends only. It can be sung in a mere whisper. The dirty room, lit by one weak and naked electric-light bulb, is full of wretched, ill-looking men; the proprietor wanders round with a bottle of white wine in his hand filling up glasses. In one corner four men are sitting, with their heads close together, and one notices that one of them is strumming quietly on the table and another is murmuring to himself, occasionally glancing up at his friends, who gravely nod. The finger strumming increases and at last the murmurer breaks into one low word, singing it under the breath in the falsetto voice of the gypsies. "*Ay*," he sings. Or "*Leli, Leli*," prolonging the note like a drawn-out sigh, and when he stops, the strumming of the fingers becomes more rapid, building up emotion and tension and obsession, until at last the low voice cries out a few words that are like an exclamation suddenly coming from some unknown person in the dark. What are the words? They are difficult to understand because the gypsies and, indeed, the Andalusians, drop so many consonants from their words that the speech sounds like a mouthful of small pebbles rubbed against one another:

> *Cada vez que considero*
> *Que me tengo que mori*

the voice declaims:

> "Whenever I remember that I must die—"

wavering on its words and then suddenly ending; and the strumming begins again until the rapid climax of the song,

Tiendo la capa en el suelo
Y me jarto de dormi

"I spread my cloak on the ground
And fling myself to sleep."

The manners of the thieves' kitchen are correct and unmarred by familiarity. A yellow-haired and drunken prostitute may be annoying a man by rumpling his hair, but otherwise the dejected customers at three in the morning are sober. One night, in a place like this in the middle of Madrid, we sat next to one of these private artists who was murmuring away to his friends. When we nodded our admiration to the whispering singer, he sang a polite love song of delightful conceit to the lady in our party and asked afterwards for "the loan of a cigarette until next Thursday." He became obviously impatient of a gypsy singer and guitarist who had smelt us out. He objected, on the usual Spanish grounds, that the young singer—who also danced—was not keeping to the rigid requirements of his art, and was introducing unclassical extravagance and stunts in order to show off to foreigners. The criticism was audible. The gypsy, egged on by criticism, scornfully tried to surpass himself. He had a weak chest and was inclined to be wild and raucous on his top notes, but he was not bad. Finding himself still mocked by the quiet man in the corner, the gypsy decided to silence him by a crushing performance, which meant a display of whirling fury. He moved one or two chairs, to make room to dance in: the customers murmured at this move. They were prepared to put up with it and hold their hand. But when the gypsy started taking off his jacket—the supreme symbol of male respectability in Spain—there was that alarming and general shout of "*¡Eso no!*"—"None of *that!*"—from everyone in the room, and half the men stood up. The proprietor rushed out at him. The gypsy put back his jacket. He knew he had gone too far.

Performances of this kind, in which some players fasten themselves on the tourist and give their performance, are usually paid for with a bottle of brandy and a cigarette or two; or, in smarter surroundings when there is a special invitation, by money. One pays up and hopes for the best, but we had a large, quiet Yorkshireman in our party whose air of Saxon shyness concealed a deep knowledge of the Spanish vernacular and an obstinate respect for correct procedure. Our young gypsy made the error of asking the Yorkshireman a special fee because he was a professional artist giving an unusual performance, and when this was refused there was a characteristic row. It began on the doorstep of the cellar, continued in the street, trailed down to the middle of the Puerta del Sol. It was a hot night; the clock on the Ministry of the Interior coldly struck four, while the gypsy shouted, the Yorkshireman argued back. The gypsy called for witnesses. At four in the morning the recognized authority of the streets is the night watchmen. They came out one by one from their doorways like the Watch of Fielding's London, and with them the strange night population who sleep out in doorways or the streets. The gypsy stuck out his chest, produced his official papers. The crowd listened. A woman, a lottery-ticket seller, recommended going to the police station, and on the whole the crowd were against us, until the gypsy made a fatal mistake of overplaying his hand. From his papers he picked out some document.

"I am an artist," he cried. They nodded sympathetically.

"I was a soldier of Franco," he added, showing more papers. They stepped back from him at once.

"None of that," someone said politely.

Among the common people of Madrid one is not likely to get very far with being a soldier of Franco.

The dispute now left the chest-baring, chest-thumping, and paper-showing stage, to insults like:

"You are boring me. Go away."

"On the contrary, it is you who are boring me."

The quarrel trailed off to the police station, but

within sight of it the gypsy gave in. It was now the time for face-saving. The gypsy said he had no wish to quarrel. The Yorkshireman said he loved the greatness of the Spanish nation. The gypsy said he loved the greatness of the English nation. A year later I was astonished to see my friends had engaged this gypsy to sing again. He had a young wife now. The gypsy was not at all surprised. Such rows are common in Spain.

"It is better," he said, "to begin a friendship with a little aversion."

His wife, a little round thing of sixteen, eight months pregnant and with pretty eyes as dark as linseed, sat with the dignity of a little duchess on her chair. She sang with the wit and grace of an angel one moment, and the next could let out the gutter howl of her race and the distorted vowels of her tongue, with the resonance of a hammer on the anvil. Strong, good-humoured and quick to catch the slightest allusion in talk, she had already acquired that matriarchal force, militancy, and content characteristic of Spanish women, and her young husband, ill from the grim night-life of the streets and bars, anxious and excitable, seemed superior to her only in his power of indifference.

As the singer of *cante flamenco* proceeds, his friends nod and wait for him to reach the few difficult orna-

133

mental notes of the little song, which has been sung
entirely for this short crisis of virtuosity. It breaks
suddenly, and then the voice flows cleverly away, to
the murmurs of *Olé*, *Olé*, by his friends. After a long
interval, in which all seem to be savouring the satisfaction the song has given them, one of the others
takes his turn and so, in this low whispering, like mus-
ing aloud or like grief and sobs, they will pass their
evenings.

Cante hondo or *cante flamenco* is not commonly
heard in this quiet fashion. The Spaniards love noise,
and the singing is usually done at the top of the voice,
but the same collusive demeanour of the party will be
observed. They listen, nodding, seeming to be waiting
for some unknown, intimate moment; an audience
will go on talking with indifference, at the beginning
of a song, for they are interested only in the few
bars that test the singer. They react to every syllable
of that passage and when the singer has reached it,
when the most tortured ornament the voice can utter
is before him, they fall dead silent as they do at some
high moment of the bullfight. The peculiarity of a
cante hondo is that it is sung within "a compass which
rarely exceeds the limits of a sixth, which is not
composed solely of nine semitones" (I quote from
Trend's translation of Falla's work on the subject) "as
is the case with our tempered scale. By the employ-

134

ment of the enharmonic genus, there is a considerable increase in the number of tones which the singer can produce." Metrical feeling is often destroyed and one seems to be listening to a sudden, lyrical or passionate statement or exclamation, torn out of the heart of the singer.

Cante hondo is the name given to this kind of singing in its pure form. *Cante flamenco* is the modern popular name for it and covers its more florid variations. The word *"flamenco"* is a mysterious word, literally meaning Flemish, which has come to mean popular, vulgar, exuberant. A loud and free behaviour —for Spaniards usually comport themselves with gravity and reserve—is called *"muy flamenco."* The word is half abusive, half indulgent, and is thought to have come in when Charles V brought his Flemish court to Spain. The Spaniard, who has always derided foreigners and blamed all his misfortunes on them, thought of the Flemings as outlandish. *Flamenco* singing has been despised in the past and it has only become common all over Spain since Falla held a congress of *flamenco* singers in Granada in 1922, when he was exploring the history and growth of Spanish folk music.

What the world outside of Spain regards as "typically Spanish music" was fixed in the 1880's of the last century by *Carmen*, a manifestation of the romantic view of Spain fostered by Gautier and Mérimée and other French writers. It really has its roots in the eighteenth century. There is a good deal of street music and the barrel organ in it, but in fact *Carmen* has one or two indigenous Spanish things to say, as Trend points out. The Spanish idiom came out in the *zarzuelas* or musical comedies of the century; there are traces of it in the seventeenth century and there are motifs that have been traced back to the songs sung by the shepherds of Castile in the fifteenth century. The interesting thing is that one of the orchestral interludes from *Carmen* is really an Andalusian *polo*, and a *polo* is really *canate hondo*.

But *cante hondo* is not like the rest of Spanish folk music, which recalls the gay, gracious, tinkling folk songs of Russia, and indeed of all European countries. The words often amusingly convey a purely Spanish foible. *Cante hondo* is Andalusian, but it is not Andalusian folk music which has felt the influence of the Byzantine liturgy and of the Moors. *Cante hondo* is gypsy; it has a lot in common with Indian singing. It contains the melancholy, the fury, the lyrical and tragic feeling of that wandering race. Though it may be sung at some gypsy feast, with the old gypsy gripping the bars of his chair outside his cave dwelling, as he mouths his way towards the notes, the prolonged and tortured "a's" and "o's," the "l" turned into an "*r*," the effect is of soliloquy, an utterance out of lone-

liness, an utterance of tragic memory, hate, vengeance,
or derision. Some are, indeed, called *soleares* (the
Spanish word *soledades* in the gypsy pronunciation),
songs of solitude:

> *Le dijo er tiempo ar quere:*
> *Esa soberbia que tienes*
> *Yo te la castigare*

> Let me tell you now we are making love—
> I will punish this pride of yours

Some, simply *coplas*, or verses:

> *Er tambo es tu retrato;*
> *Que mete mucho ruio*
> *Y si se mira por dentro*
> *S'ecuentra qu'esta basio*

> This drum is just like you:
> It makes a loud noise.
> But look inside—it is empty!

> *Si la Inquisicion supiera*
> *Lo mucho que t'he querio*
> *Y er mai pago que m'has dao*
> *Te quemaban por judio*

> If the Inquisition had known
> How much I loved you
> And the bad coin in which you paid me for it
> They would have burned you for a Jew.

Falla organized his congress in Granada thirty years ago in order to preserve *cante hondo*, and spoke of its "grave, hieratic melody." Hieratic it is; in another form, the *saeta*, it is sung to convey the agony of religious desire and remorse, as the images of the Christ or the Virgin are borne round the white-walled streets of Seville in the nights of Holy Week. But the modern tendency has been to get away from the severe, classical design of this pattern of sound which seems to cut the southern night like a knife, to stir in one animal feelings of fear, cruelty, and pity. The more florid, rasping, less inhibited *flamenco* versions are replacing the older form. One hears a good deal too much of the nasal howl let out in a voice that whines and strains the blood vessels. The Spanish voice is harsh, powerful, and dry, as if there were sand in the singer's throat, in any case. Impatient of restraint, the Spanish popular arts are quickly spoiled by exuberance. Spanish fury, when it is aroused in life or simulated in art, is terrifying, for it is carried to the limit of frenzy. Nothing grips the Spaniards so much as the dancer whirling herself into a state of mad, dishevelled passion, and the gypsies are unsurpassed in these transports and climaxes of abandon.

One has only to go to the theatre or to any display of dancing in Spain to see how actors and dancers come onto the stage, not as artists—even though they

may be good artists—but as persons. They recognize
friends in the audience, wave to them or smile to them
indiscreetly in the middle of their performance, with
a slackness and an indolence towards the discipline of
their art which is provincial and amateur. It is hard for
them to sink the person in the artist; they are incurable
and obstinate human beings. Yet the opposite tendency
is there—an exact, indeed pedantic knowledge of the
castizo or classical canon, and if the singer or the
dancer fails in one single particular of what he ought
to do, the audience rises at once—and I mean rises—
they get to their feet and shout *"No"* and cry abuse
and irony, as they do at the bullfight when the bullfighter makes even a minor error.

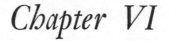

Chapter VI

There are two roads to the south: one straight
across the tableland of La Mancha, with the
sharp mountains burning and floating like crisp blue
gas flame on the horizon; the other, the long way
round, over the Gredos mountains into the sheep
drives, the wilderness, the cork woods of Extremadura, where the large estates begin. The river Tagus
lies green as a snake in its deep ravines in this country;
in the oasis of Aranjuez it is muddy; at Toledo the
river circles the town like some green viper in its
gorge.

La Mancha is Don Quixote's country. Under a sun

of brass it is greener than old Castile, for the short
vines grow here mile after mile, the pony turns the
waterwheel under the trees, and the villages and towns
are white, single-storey places. Valdepeñas is a wine
town; this wine and the heavier wines of Rioja in the
north are the best-known wines of the country. There
are no vintages and no châteaux. One takes the wine
of the locality, some of it delicate, some of it tasting
of the pine cask like the wines of Greece, some of it
thin and sour. "This is the best wine in the world,"
people say. And they say the same of the water, which
is generally pure, crystalline, and excellent. After
Valdepeñas the soil reddens. The heat comes down
on the earth like a crushing load, the people stare
under the weight of the sun, the women fan themselves and sigh. We travel in the strong smell of the
earth and its herbs, the scented smell of the soft-coal
smoke, sweet human sweat, face powder, urine. In
the towns the odours of olive oil, charcoal, and polish
stand, almost like persons themselves, in the cold doorways of the hot streets. The olive groves begin, strip-
ing and furring the red hills for mile after mile, and in
such wealth it is hard to understand Spanish poverty.
We see those thin, crumpled-up monkey peasants,
those lean and noble-looking people; we see the ex-
traordinary division of Spain between them and the
bland, unlined faces of the fat, who carry their bellies

like terrestrial globes before them, whose chins appear like motor tires under the jaws, whose small eyes have the innocence, the surprise, the resignation, and the malice of the obese. It is a country divided between those who eat well and those who do not, and when you talk about the next town to a countryman there is always the gesture of the fingers to the mouth: "There they eat well." Or "Here we do not eat." And by "well" they mean quantity. Since the war—"*no se come*"—there is nothing to eat; how many scores of times I have heard those words! "Eat"—it is the governing Spanish word; *mañana* is nowhere near it. We are always brought down to the fundamentals of life; he eats well; he does not; here I conducted my love affairs; there I have my family; my parents are dead; my parents are alive; life is sad; life is gay; I am alive; people manage to live. Rich people. Unfortunate people. Lucky and unlucky: the passing words of Spanish life display the primitive dichotomy of good and evil chance. One might be listening to the Bible.

Just as the Pancorbo Pass in the north takes one onto the tableland, so the pass through the Sierra Morena drops one off it into the lower hills and plains of the south and Andalusia, out of the dry tingling air into an air that is softer and sweet as syrup. The mild winter and the early spring give a brief greenness to this country. By June the sun has scorched it up. The dry Spain, where the rainfall is poor, is fertile only by its slow rivers, and here the Guadalquivir crawls to Córdoba and Seville on its green plain. The cactus appears, like thick green cardboard on the roadside, and the spears of the aloes. Grey donkeys trot on the roads. The herds of little black goats tinkle on the wasteland and circle in the shade of the long avenues of eucalyptus. At Córdoba the green oranges are on the trees. Yet although the country looks soft and rich, this is the region of huge estates and casual, wretchedly paid labour. We are in the region of serfdom, the Spanish Russia of the nineteenth century. No people in Spain more gracious, none poorer than the peasantry of large areas of Andalusia; yet none more disposed, by traditional character, to finding the minimum that will support life.

Andalusia is what for a century or more the foreigner has understood to be Spain. It is the Spain of the romantic legend, as Castile is the Spain of the "black legend," *la leyenda negra*. We see in our mind's eye the Córdoba hat of the Feria, the women with the high combs, the proud carriage, and the rose or carnation in their hair; we see the dangerous gypsy dancer, the long-toothed, narrow-hipped bullfighter, the figure of Don Juan. We see the cool tiled patios of Córdoba, Seville, and Granada, hear the lazy talking of the guitar, the electric crackle of castanets, as the twisting arms swing down. We are in the heart of the Moorish kingdom and have one foot in the East. Flowers, singing, sunlight, black shade, and the rustle of water.

Is it like this? Shall we be deceived? No—as always in Spain, if we look at one face it is like this; the face turns and we see the opposite. Romantic Andalusia was an invention of the French, especially of Théophile Gautier, Mérimée, and, later, of Maurice Barrès; the country of *"Le sang, la volupté, et la mort,"* and in the enchantment of Holy Week in Seville those ideas easily catch the northern imagination. Nor must we underrate them: the French are more intelligent and imaginative than the Spaniards, and have simply prolonged certain Andalusian characteristics into a higher key and turned them into general ideas.

The traveller who goes by the Extremadura road into Andalusia, through Trujillo, where Cortés was born, and on to Plasencia, pretty Cáceres with its garrison, and Badajoz, has a sight of the real army that Castile sent out to attack the economy of southern Spain. He will see the survival of the *mesta,* the large migratory flocks of sheep slowly moving south or north according to the season. One sits under the cork trees of the wilderness talking to the shepherds. Spare, austere men, they wear tooled leather aprons over their trouser legs and carry the crook and the horn slung on their shoulders. Formed by the lonely life, they speak with majestic yet simple courtliness to strangers in a clear sagacious Castilian of complete purity. It is delivered slowly.

"Man! How are you? And how are your family? Is your wife well? Are your children well? I am glad. You are right to rest in the heat. If God does not want to send the rain, one may complain above, below, everywhere, but that will not make the rain come."

"What do you think of life?"

"Nothing."

"Nothing?"

"Nothing. When one eats well, good. When one eats badly—well, good too. One remains living until one is put into the ground. Then nothing, man—nothing."

The white dust of the flocks clouds on the roads, and before the motor-car came in, whenever one saw a cloud of dust on the Castilian tracks it was made by the flocks of sheep. The flocks of the *mesta*, the great enemies of the dying farmer, and the enemies of Andalusia, were the sheep charged by Don Quixote when he thought they were an army led by hostile knights. In his madness, Don Quixote was right. When wool ousted silk as the profitable product—and the Arabs introduced the merino sheep into Spain—the famous wool monopoly of the *mesta* was founded in Castile, and Andalusian ruin was complete.

In his analysis of the condition of Andalusia in *The Spanish Labyrinth*, Gerald Brenan points out that until the coming of the industrial age the history of Spain can be dramatized as a struggle of the rich agricultural districts of Andalusia and the eastern or Mediterranean regions against semi-pastoral Castile. Córdoba, Seville, Málaga, and Almería—that now forgotten little Manchester frying in the heat of its pothole among the mountains of the coast—were rich industrial cities: the decline began when the cities of northern Europe, waking up from the Middle Ages, set up factories of their own. The semi-pastoral Spaniards of Castile were then able to conquer Andalusia and the south. It is the old story of trade and war. By the seventeenth century, huge tracts of once fertile country had reverted to wilderness. The Venetian ambassador observed the decline in the enormously rich province of Granada only thirty-four years after Granada was taken from the Moors in 1492. He wrote:

Hidden among them [the waters, fruit, trees, woods] are the farms of the Moors, many in ruins, for the Moorish population is diminishing and it is they who kept everything in order; the Spaniards here, as in other parts of Spain, are not industrious and disdain work.

And Brenan enlarges on the political effects of this economic change:

The shepherds wage a perpetual war on the agriculturalists, whom they regard as their inferiors, whilst both together feel a fierce envy of the city dwellers and cultivators of rich oases. . . . Now this is a type of society which is not confined to Spain but appears wherever certain climatic conditions prevail. It is strongly developed in Persia and North Africa. One of its chief characteristics is its instability; it alternates violently between a centralised tyranny and an anarchic tribal or local life. With every bad drought or economic crisis there is either a revolution or a wave of religious exaltation, whilst at longer intervals there are great upheavals in which all the energies of the country are poured out in a war of conquest, leaving it inert and exhausted afterwards. . . . The famous orientalism of the Spaniards is not due to "Arab blood," but to climate and geography.

In the seventeenth and eighteenth centuries there were attempts to deal with agriculture on collectivist lines—they were revived under the Spanish Republic of 1931 and abolished by General Franco—but the Napoleonic invasion put an end to reform. By the 1830's and '40's, the sale of the Church land and common lands led to a revival of capitalist agriculture; the land went out of the hands of the small owners into the hands of the large ones; the number of huge estates in Andalusia increased, falling mostly into the hands of a new rich class, who reduced the Andalusian peasant to the level of a labour force, miserably paid, controlled by the bailiffs, and kept down, when they protested, by the Civil Guard. There is a parallel in the condition of England during the industrial revolution. In Spain, likewise, the fortunes of the new middle class were made; a large class of absentee landlords was formed, and if one asks why one's friend X can spend all day sitting doing nothing in a café in Seville or Córdoba, or lie in bed all day in Madrid, to get up and talk and play cards with his friends all night, the answer is in the rush to buy the Church and common land cheap in the nineteenth century, and the profitable result.

Serfdom is behind the strength of the anarcho-syndicalist movement in Andalusia, the periodical riots, crop-burnings, the savage scenes of the Civil War, the fact that the only place in Spain where Communism, also, had a small hold was near Seville. After Córdoba one sees the palm huts or kraal-like villages of the peasants, the slums made of beaten-out petrol tins; the esparto grows where the crops ought to grow. And in this region 41 per cent of the land—and the best—is owned by the big estates, and further south in Seville and Cádiz the figure rises to 58 per cent. The wages paid to the seasonal labourers are derisory and their conditions of life and work intolerable. The foreigner has only to stop and talk to any working man, especially in the south, to find himself suddenly surrounded by a dozen more and in the midst of a violent political meeting, though such discussions are forbidden under the Franco regime.

In Almería, last year, a group of ten fine fellows, naked to the waist, thin and lithe, put down their picks and rushed at me.

"Why do you come here? To look at our misery? Do people eat well in your country? Here we starve. How can one keep a wife and children on twelve pesetas a day?" (The wages seem to range from 12 to 18 pesetas; that is, at the present exchange about $2.10 to $2.80 a week.)

They blow up with mocking rage. Their eyes look not with hostility but with astonished curiosity at one's respectable clothes. These men are well informed about conditions in other countries. They do not whine or threaten; in their excitability they do not lose human dignity or good manners. Unlike the Russian peasants who lived (or live) under the same conditions, the Spaniards are not soaked in drink, for they drink very little, and rarely spirits. (The aguardiente is the drink of the carters in the roadside taverns, not the drink of the ordinary worker.) Some show of providing social services has indeed been made by the Franco regime, but one of the first steps of Franco was to give back the land to those landlords who had been expropriated under the Republic; and no serious attempt has been made to deal with the terrible fundamental problem: how to support a huge and growing population by farming in a dry climate is the essence of it. The traveller is, of course, told that the condition of Andalusia is due to the idleness of the people in this soft climate, and it is true that in the towns one can see hordes of idle people. They belong to two groups: people content to live on their small rents and the large numbers of unemployed. Those who work are working hard.

When one eats the Andalusian *gazpacho*, that ice-cold soup of cucumber and tomatoes and peppers ground up in vinegar and oil, in the cool, darkened room of the pension in Seville or Córdoba, and after that the fish done in oil, the squids, the hakes and brill, and then the thin steaks or the chicken, one recalls that out in the palmetto kraals the poor man has eaten *gazpacho* alone; cold in the middle of the day, hot at night, and that the dish will be not much more than bread dipped into a dish of oil and vinegar.

The Andalusians are very different in general character from the Spaniards of Castile. They do not lisp the letter "c" or "z" in their speech; they drop out as many consonants as possible from their words and speak fast in shouting, headlong voices as if their

mouths were full of marbles. They are very difficult
to understand. They are gay, full of smiles and laughter in their talk, a frivolous and light-hearted people.
They pride themselves on verbal wit and an allusive-
ness so fine and constant that the mind has to work at
double speed to keep up with their fancifulness, their
hyperbole, their mocking, and their sparkling conceit
of themselves. Sedate Castilians regard the Andalusians
as buffoons, without gravity or reserve; they are certainly nervous, naïve, easily happy, easily carried up
and down by their feeling. They live in the minute.
Their effervescence is delightful, their compliments
are unending. Everyone seems to be a minor lyrical
poet or a story-teller. They are as quick as the Irish
with a phrase. Only in Naples—a city long under
Spanish dominion, whose dialect is full of Spanish
turns of phrase—does one find something like the nature of the people of Seville. Yet Andalusia is also the
home of the philosophers. The vice of these people
who pride themselves on their gaiety and sparkle is
avarice and stinginess. No one parts with a penny
more reluctantly. Another weakness is for the cruel
or dangerous practical joke; they love horseplay at
the expense of strangers. Their religion is almost pagan, and they are less puritan than the Castilians in
love. There are vestiges of the Moorish harem system
in Andalusian life; it is not very uncommon to find

men who have fathered two or three families and who solemnly go the rounds of them—a tolerated manner of living which is rare elsewhere in Spain, though—in true Spanish fashion—the habit is domestic, patriarchal, and connubial rather than licentious.

Deep personal reserve and formality combine, in the paradoxical Spanish fashion, with immediate easy familiarity, in most parts of Spain. In Andalusia the familiarity is more evident than the reserve. The servant slaps the fly on the master's shoulder, the people in the street call out to the image of the Virgin as it is borne down the street in the processions at Holy Week, as if she were a girl of the neighbourhood; no one can contain the amount of talk that is idling away inside him. One is surrounded by intimates who unbosom at once and pass off, forgetting you and what they said, in a moment.

One knows all the south, and Seville above all, by the slowness of the pace of people walking. Long before midday, when Easter has passed, the awnings are pulled over the streets like Sierpes, where no traffic is allowed to drive, and the cafés and clubs are packed with men. They are drinking sherry and eating prawns and shellfish. The women who regard themselves of any account rarely leave their homes till five in the afternoon, and the horse carriages, with their red-spoked wheels, are nearly as common as the taxis.

The Spanish Temper

One is back in the nineteenth century, though the new parts of Seville are modern enough.

In the Barrio Santa Cruz one walks streets that are hardly more than two yards wide, and the white-walled houses have the grille windows, the wrought-iron gates that lead into the cool courtyards where the ferns stand round the fountains. The privacy of these places is mysterious. They are houses made for a life lived in the shade or for the long conversations of the night, and as the year advances, in all of Spain, the long cool night reanimates people. It becomes a country where the whole population of the towns sits under the trees or slowly walks there in the strange solitude of Spaniards or in their loud, shouting, interminable conversations. These barred windows recall the pictures of the cloaked lover standing there and talking for hours to the young woman shut up within. I have not seen this happen for twenty years; the Civil War was a revolution.

Writing in the eighteenth century, Cadalso, a Spanish commentator on social customs, said that in general the Spaniards had an "excessive propensity for love." He was writing in a period of public licence, the time of the *cortejos* (or *cicebeos*), when, in imitation of the French, the stern duties of Spanish jealousy were relaxed, at any rate in the smart circles of the great cities. The Spaniards have often been credited with

this excessive propensity by romantically minded foreigners, and Seville is, after all, the city of Don Juan.
Fashions in morals change very frequently and it
would be absurd to generalize and invent a "Spanish
attitude to love"; but there is no doubt that the Andalusians have a gift for the poetical admiration of
women and a considerable vanity in being thought
pursuers and admirers. This warmth of temperament
is an obligation to self-respect and is possibly a response to the segregation of women. Slowly this segregation is weakening, but even when segregation has
ceased, its effect on manners still remains. Don Juan
himself is a figure created in response to this separation
of the sexes, and has also a sadistic side which perhaps
comes from the excesses of the court of Philip IV in
the seventeenth century, when some of the convents
had fallen into disorder. The love affair with a nun,
the murder of a wife whose honour had been perhaps
innocently compromised, were popular fantasies of
sexual violence. Spanish inhibition or love of extremity
created these fantasies. The public scourgings of heretics, infidels, or penitents lasted well into the eighteenth century and indicate the tastes of a violent
people.

Don Quixote, the deluded Castilian knight, and Don
Juan, the inexhaustible and ruthless Andalusian lover,
are the two great mythical figures which Spain has

given to the world. Both are armed and warlike men; both are exemplars of the imagination attempting to impose itself upon reality. Don Quixote attempts to impose the vision of the romances of chivalry. He is defeated, and many serious readers have been tempted —as I have already said—to regard the tale as a tragic comment on the Spanish knightly adventure in the Counter-Reformation and the conquest of America. Don Quixote has been called the book that killed a nation by cutting away the illusion that was necessary to its life. The answer to this is that the decay had already begun by the time of Cervantes. Outside of Spain, Don Quixote is seen as an eccentric, a saint, a deluded idealist upon whom the sceptical realism of Sancho Panza makes the irreverent comment of reality. These elements can indeed be perceived in *Don Quixote*, but there is something subtler in the portrait. Don Quixote enacts not the tragedy of idealism or vision, but the condition of the imagination itself, which both illumines and darkens the mind. The story contains the mind's knowledge of its own hallucinatory nature. The great heights of the book are reached when the sly shafts of sanity light up the twilight of Don Quixote's mind, when he appears to know his own folly, but does so only to plunge deeper. Death alone can cure him, and the irony is that it is Sancho, the squire, who returns like a hero, for he at least has governed an island. Yet even he has been deceived: we have seen a parable not of the condition of Spain, but of the condition of human life. The extreme strains of the Spanish nature are celebrated in these two characters: the passionate tendency to fantasy, the fatal reaction into scepticism, realism, and cynicism.

Don Juan, on the other hand, is an example of the imagination imposing itself successfully upon reality, but failing to conquer death, for in the earliest play about Don Juan, by Tirso de Molina, where the character first appears, Don Juan goes down in the cold grip of the Commendador's stone hand, to eternal torment. In the romantic nineteenth-century play by Zorrilla, he is rescued for heaven by the pure love of Doña Inés. Because Don Juan always succeeds, he is not a character of any complexity, which Don Quixote is—indeed, he is hardly a character at all—but a universal day-dream or myth. He expresses the male desire for inexhaustible sexual vitality, the female desire to be ravished against the will, reason, interest, or honour. He embodies an aspect of male anarchism and the desire for absolute power.

Although a Spanish playwright was the first to create Don Juan, modern Spanish critics deny—with strong reason—that he is a human being and that he is a Spaniard in any special sense at all. There is a paradox in this disowning of Don Juan, and it is

interesting to examine it. The character of Don Juan
has had a far greater development outside of Spain,
in Mozart, in Molière, possibly in Richardson's Love-
lace, obviously in Byron; but whenever the Italians,
in their researches into the Italian theatre of Tirso's
time, have claimed him, Spanish patriotism and schol-
arship are affronted. (See Ramiro de Maeztu's essay
on the subject.) The second thing to notice is that if
Spanish intellectuals have rejected Don Juan, the common people have not. The Don Juan they accept is
not the original figure of Tirso de Molina, but the
romantic, melodramatic, and Frenchified Don Juan of
the nineteenth century invented by the dramatist Zorrilla. Zorrilla's *Don Juan Tenorio* is played every year
on All Souls' Eve in most Spanish cities, and it has
become a popular ritual rather like the annual reading
of Dickens's *Christmas Carol* at Christmas in England.
The packed audience knows the famous lines by heart.
The famous moment when Don Juan describes how
he nails up his truculent notice on the door of his
house, saying: "Here lives Don Juan Tenorio and if
any man wants anything of him . . ." have become a
proverbial satire of Spanish defiance. Don Juan's is an
act which, in some form or other, every Spaniard
dreams of performing, and in fact in his inner life is
doing all the time. He is asserting the exclusive, dramatic rights of the human ego—myself before all other

selves, unrepentantly. Yet, though the people respond
to this aspect of Don Juan, the intellectual critics are
right in pointing out that, even in Andalusia, Don Juan
does not embody a specifically Spanish conception.
There is little or no literature of gallantry in Spain;
there is no book to compare with the *Liaisons dangereuses*. In the picaresque story of the Archpriest of
Hita, either love is carnal or it is the love of the Virgin,
and even the most decorous never think of disguising
the carnality of love. As Spaniards see everything in
black and white, the Stendhalian categories of love are
a refinement they ignore or reprehend. Whatever else
he is, Don Juan is not an epicurean.

It is difficult to know when Don Juan is Spanish—
for he was, at any rate, created a Spaniard—and when
he is simply a universal wish. Tirso de Molina's play
was written in the very early seventeenth century. It
is called *El Burlador de Sevilla*—the mocker of Seville, not, it will be noted, the lover—for Don Juan is
an Andalusian in his love of the preposterous fantasy,
of laughing at his enemies, and of succeeding by boast
and effrontery and trick. He is a picaresque character
turned hero. In the first act of the play we see him in
his typical situation. The scene is at night. Don Juan
has entered the Duchess Isabel's room in the Royal
Palace at Naples, and, persuading her in the dark that
he is her betrothed, has seduced her. Not a very great

feat: she had probably never seen her future husband. She longs to see her lover's face and moves to get a lamp. Don Juan stops her. She suspects at once and asks, in terror: "What man are you?" Don Juan replies: "A man without a name." She cries for help, and when the King and the guards come in shouting: "Who is there?" Don Juan answers dryly: "A man and a woman—what else could it be?" Male and female: the world narrowed down to sex, to the primitive human situation. It is a sentence that smashes the elaborate Spanish marriage system at a blow. Man, woman, culminating in the sexual act: it is the basic meaning of so many of the Spanish dances, which are patterns not of romantic or gracious beguilement but of the phases of sexual challenge. There is as much hatred as there is love in these incitements, and they create the hallucination by which passion is built up and released. In this episode of Tirso's play, the most destructive and unflinching male who will stop at nothing has met the most difficult, the least accessible woman. Don Juan owes it to his honour to break the established codes of honour—to attack the royal Duchess, the friend's betrothed, the bride on her wedding day, the innocent girl who rescues him and saves his life, the novice in the convent. Speed, trickery— he wins easily by simple promise of marriage—the killing of any opponent, and the quick get-away sum up the process. "I'll have her tonight"—once he has said that, his "I" is committed. Nothing can be allowed to stand in the way of what he owes to his own pride. He is the national intransigence isolated.

The Don Juan of Tirso de Molina is a liar, a deceiver, a betrayer of friends, a brawler and murderer. He has one virtue: absolute fearlessness. What drives him on is pride and the idea of the greater difficulty. He claims total freedom and unlimited energy for enjoying it; no law of diminishing returns operates upon his desires. And he is good-humoured and a great mocker; his wit and recklessness fascinate his friends— Benavente, a contemporary dramatist, has shrewdly pointed out that Don Juan puts such a lasting spell upon the men to whom he boasts that the women hardly see him—as for the eternal punishment, that is "a long way off." He is not afraid of the dead and not respectful to sacred places: he pulls the stone beard of the Commendador's statue in the chapel, and it is he who has murdered the Commendador. Above all, he is a figure of the night. "Why are you in my room at this hour of night!" exclaims one victim. "These hours above all are my hours," Don Juan replies.

Out of their context such satanic lines have an absurd ring, for we can only imagine an unreal, melodramatic figure speaking them. But, clearly, Don Juan is not a person, and in their context such lines are arresting. They are spoken not by a human being but by a demon, and those hours of darkness are, indeed, the kingdom of the carnal spirit.

In Tirso de Molina's play Don Juan does not love any woman. He merely possesses women. He is a ravisher—though by deceit, not by violence. His victims are left in tears and grief, for his promises are broken. We can indulge in speculations about the secret pleasure these women have in the irresistible, grief-dealing lover, but nothing in the play justifies us, and indeed Tirso accepts the common experience that the demands of the male ego are different from those of the female. In his long essay Ramiro de Maeztu makes the good point that there are two Don Juans: the Don Juan who appears north of the Pyrenees, who is the romantic rebel, the endless seeker of an ideal love, discarding because he has not found it; and the Don Juan of the south, who is not a lover, but an animal energy or will to power. The absence of northern idealism in love, according to this writer and, indeed, to many other Spanish commentators, is very Spanish; in place of idealism there is obsession, fantasy, passion, the desire to go to the limit. Even in the love of the divine Spouse, described by Spanish mystics (and this is the only Spanish literature which can be said to be exclusively concerned with the psychology

of love), the ecstasy of ultimate union is reached by
the established processes of our sensibility, and not by
a sudden leap from the material to the spiritual world.
If a spiritual world is imagined, it is not formless,
bodiless, and metaphysical, but is conceived of in
corporeal terms. Impossible for these realists to consider a union of souls which is not, by some magic of
transubstantiation, a union of bodies. In the north,
Don Juan is saved by the discovery of ideal love; in the
south—he goes to hell in Tirso de Molina, and in Zorrilla's play he is saved by the chaste intercession of
Doña Inés, which is a bow to northern romantic senti-
ment. Doña Inés does succeed in awakening love in
Don Juan, and in doing so turns him into a recogniza-
ble human being. The result is that he diminishes at
once. But she has been able to do this because she is
hardly more than a child, and may be considered as
emotionally immature or unborn, as Don Juan is. She
is, emotionally speaking, his similar and match. But, in
fact, Maeztu's generalizations about the northern
and the southern Don Juan are not quite exact: Love-
lace in Richardson's *Clarissa*, and Valmont in the
Liaisons dangereuses, are two hard militant Don Juans
who seek no ideal woman. Their aim, like that of the
Spanish Don Juan, is the destruction of the being they
are seducing, and themselves are eventually destroyed

in the personal hells they have been unconsciously preparing.

Don Juan is Spanish to the extent that he violently celebrates the implacable and unmovable *"Yo"* or *"I"* of Spanish individualism. Ganivet, who made an inquiry into the causes of Spanish decadence after the loss of Cuba in 1898, said the Spaniard was a man who carried on his passport the imaginary words "This Spaniard is authorized to do whatever he wants." Pride, courage, extremism, energy, anarchism are the Spanish substitutes for that idealism which is given to the Don Juan of the north. In Zorrilla's play, God agrees to make room for Don Juan, who, though supposedly repentant, is still shouting about his honour and is obviously going to be very troublesome in heaven.

Yet if Tirso's *Don Juan* had been simply a play about a man who runs after women, we can doubt if it would have had the myth-creating quality. The *Burlador* is really two plays in one: the story of Don Juan, the destroyer of women, is married to the old folk legend of the dead man invited to the feast. In some parts of Spain, right up to the eighteenth century, the peasants used to go to the churches on All Souls' Night to make prayers and offerings for the dead. As it was a feast day, they would often take their glasses of wine there and very soon were raising their glasses to the departed and inviting them mockingly to eat or drink. As in modern Mexico, the dead spirits were placated and kept off by comedy and mockery. Dr. Marañón, who has written with scepticism about Don Juan, says that the religious and funereal elements in the play are the only truly Spanish thing in it; the rest, he says, is simply an Italian Renaissance figure, a Borgia, or simply the gangster or condottiere. This argument is a counterattack upon those who have seen Don Juan as an example of the spirit of the Spanish conquistador. Certainly the conquistadors were governed by a great idea and represent Spanish character at its most splendid; they were not intriguers and tricksters without religion. But by the early seventeenth century the figure of the conquistador was in decline, and Don Juan could be seen as a frustrated and decadent example of the type—an example, so familiar in Spain, of the man capable of great efforts of will, who recoils cynically upon himself. Another view is that Don Juan is the lawless man and rebel who rises to the top in periods of anarchy, corruption, and irreligion. He indeed first appeared in the reign of Velásquez's Philip IV, in that brilliant and licentious court, when the huge assertion of Spanish faith in the Counter-Reformation and the conquest of America was broken. Others see in him a sceptical attack on the

accepted foundations of Spanish life; the powerful institution of the family, which breaks all lovers and
which keeps the women shut away from the world;
and an attack also on the cult of honour. In Tirso's
time the cult of honour had reached a high point of
intricacy and delicacy, and when Don Juan is shown
tricking his friends, this has been regarded as a satire
on men who professed honour like a religion and
flagrantly ignored it in practice—a satire, in short, on
the morals of "young bloods."

In recent years Don Juan has met his worst enemy—
the psychologists. They find him to be not the mature
and energetic man, but the infantile male, possibly
homosexual, possibly almost impotent or with a neurotic fear of incapacity. He is fixed in the undifferen-
tiated sexuality of adolescence. He is a myth created
for those thousands of penniless lonely Spanish males
who walk up and down the streets all night, who
never see a woman outside their own homes, who are
dominated by the all-powerful figure of the Spanish
mother. Hundreds of these unstrenuous dreamers of
love are supposed, in Madrid, to get their mild satisfac-
tions from being crushed against the girls in the trams
at the rush hour. The tramway lovers they are called:
the Spanish tongue is ruthlessly satirical.

And who *was* Don Juan? Did he exist in real life?
No one has ever found a model, but for a long time

the figure of a celebrated Sevillano, Don Miguel de Mañara, was thought to be the original. His tomb lies in the Hospice for the Poor which he founded in Seville and bears the famous inscription: "Here lie the ashes of the worst man the world has ever known." Mañara's family had Corsican blood. He cannot be the original of Don Juan, for he was not born when the play was written; he is, however, an authentic Sevillian copyist of Don Juan. For the legend is that he saw the play and went home saying: "Henceforth I shall be Don Juan." He started on a career of quarrelling and murder in the street—Don Juan, of course, is a murderer as well as a lover—and of seduction. After a terrible career he married, and the sudden death of his young wife turned him to religion. His remorse led the aristocrat to put himself at the service of the poor. In rags himself, he collected the vagabonds and starving from the street and took them to the Hospice that he had founded. He was also obsessed by the idea of death, for he collected the dead from the gallows and the streets, carrying the bodies himself and giving them Christian burial. It was a branch of that fierce, fanatical, and compulsive spirit of proselytism which had driven Spaniards to convert the Moorish remnant after the reconquest, and to save even their dead from the perils of hell. Mañara, like Don Juan, became the protagonist in a large number of gruesome death legends. He pursues a beautiful woman through street after street in Seville at night, and not until she gets to her door does she allow him to overtake her; then she turns and lifts aside her veil and he sees not a face but a grinning skull. Or, again, a woman beckons to him from a balcony, and when he mounts to her room, she has vanished; the room contains a body lying in its grave-clothes between candles. Or, walking the streets again, he meets men carrying a bier and asks them: "Whose is that body? Who has died?" They answer: "It is Don Miguel de Mañara." The corpse is himself.

The Hospice in Seville contains two pictures by Valdés Leal which Mañara commissioned. One is a picture of richly dressed skeletons. A hand dangles a balance and in one pan jewels are heaped and in the other, bones. On the velvet cloth cockroaches are crawling. The preoccupation with skeletons, skulls, and the dead in Spain recalls the similar preoccupation among the Mexican Indians. Spanish and Mexican Indian ferocity, cruelty, and regard for death were oddly matched in the conquest.

In his book on Don Juan, Dr. Marañón has a far more plausible suggestion to offer those who search for an original figure in real life. His candidate is the Duke of Villamediana. He was a magnificent of Philip IV's court, a man of gorgeous apparel such as

Velásquez painted, and supposed (until contemporary historical researches have proved it otherwise) to have been the lover of the Queen. He was a famous pursuer of women, immensely rich, a great gambler, an elegant poet, and a bullfighter, for bullfighting was originally an aristocratic sport—a knightly tourney between beautifully mounted riders and the bull. The court of Philip IV lived in a condition of scandal, and all Spain knew of Villamediana's career as an uncontrollable Renaissance figure. He was eventually assassinated, and, it was generally thought, by the King's order; but a curious fact has come out which has gone a certain way towards confirming the suspicions of the psychiatrists. Villamediana was not assassinated by the King's orders; he was not the lover of the Queen; he was killed by unknown men after he was found to be implicated in a homosexual scandal which touched a large portion of the court. Homosexuality is not common in Spain; it is certainly nothing like as common or as apparent as it is in Italy, England, Germany, or America.

The last Spanish play on Don Juan was written a year or two ago by Jacinto Benavente. Benavente is the last of a group of Spanish dramatists—Martínez Sierra and the Quintero brothers were the others—and he is now a very old man. His play was light and amusing and it suggested, as I said before, that the truth about Don Juan is that the women can never get near him, though they are longing to do so, because he is always surrounded by men who are fascinated by his stories and hope to learn a trick or two from an expert. A shrewd piece of observation—Spanish males will listen all night to the fantastic boasts and amusing inventions of a good talker who is telling of his own or someone else's adventures in love. Although he is represented as an energy in Tirso de Molina and Zorrilla, Don Juan is also unmistakably a traveller, a talker and story-teller. The boasting match in Zorrilla's play is characteristic and important. We have to agree in the end that Don Juan is not a character but a wish.

It is tempting at this point to digress in a general way into the subject of the roles of the sexes in Spanish life and into the characteristics of Spanish love. To the northerner, Spain appears to be a male-dominated society in which the women have few rights or liberties and live in a state of complete subjection. He has only to meet a few educated women among either the intellectual classes or the Europeanized aristocracy to find that many of these women hold the same view. Married women live at certain legal disadvantages in relation to their husbands: the divorce laws which had a brief reign during the Republic from 1931 until 1936 have been repealed at the instance of the Church un-

der General Franco; birth control is forbidden—
though not unknown—young women go out very
little alone and are certainly not allowed the liberty
which girls have in the rest of western Europe or
America. Twenty-five years ago no nice young
woman went to the cinema with a young man unless
a duenna or another girl went too. This has changed,
but the duenna still survives in disembodied form. The
key to the Spanish love affair is the scene enacted
every Sunday afternoon in the less frequented alleys
of the parks in the big cities, and can be said to have
its counterpart in the life of all classes. Seated on a chair
with its back to a thick hedge is a young woman. Exactly in front of her sits the young man, his knees a
respectful number of inches from hers. Occasionally
his hand ventures towards her hands, there may be a
fluttering touch of the tips of the fingers for a moment,
but hers are expertly withdrawn; rarely is a hand held,
almost never is an arm put round a waist or a kiss
exchanged. If there is a kiss it will be upon the cheek,
not the mouth—this is true, of course in all Latin
countries, where to kiss on the mouth publicly is
considered an obscene act. It causes catcalls in the
cinema. And then one observes that the lovers have
brought with them a third chair. Nothing is on it, no
one sits there. The chair is a piece of conventional
stage furniture; it is meant to represent the imaginary

duenna. To an extrememly critical neighbour it might indicate that a chaperon was there a minute ago or is in fact expected. The Spanish love affair requires this fiction.

Spain is the country of long engagements that go on for years. This is the custom and it arises chiefly because of economic difficulties. In order that its interest shall not be exhausted, the engagement is kept lively on the girl's part by all the devices of reproach, hurt feelings, feigned jealousy, coldness, coquetry, and reprobation, which are overcome by infinite small attentions, presents, punctiliousness—the whole armoury of the Victorian love affair. From the man the woman demands not passion but marriage; in the woman the man sees the future mother, the image of the mother who has dominated his life so far and who, until the end of her days, will be the ruling figure in his life. His future wife knows this and is not discountenanced. She will have the same role when her large family is born. Both parties will hope to have a very large family. Monogamy is the fixed principle, and although many Spanish men like, in the interest of *amour-propre* to pretend otherwise, their attitude to sex is puritan and strict. They are deeply shocked by the enticements and behaviour of foreign women. It is a puritanism which is made emotional by the sense of honour and by continuous jealousy. These are a variable quantity from period to period in Spanish life, but in some degree they are always there.

Some Spanish writers have thought that the austerity or conventionality in Spanish love, its privacy too, contain a certain element of brutality or crudity. In times of notorious licence there is certainly something crude about the scandals of the convent, and the popular imagination runs easily to the thought of orgy. In any case, the classic Spanish attitude to love is maintained only by the preservation of the brothel and a very large population of prostitutes.

"And now," says the complacent young lady at the window to her lover as he goes off, "I suppose you are going off with one of the naughty women." To preserve the conventional façade and the bourgeois Catholic morality, one has to have the imitation domestic world of the brothel. The great poverty of the masses in Spain has enormously increased prostitution, but Spaniards are not indignant about that. Passive, fatalistic, they accept the brothel and the prostitute as an ineluctable part of life, accept them with charity, pleasure, and indulgence.

The unabashed candour of the Spaniards, men and women, in their conversations about sexual love and the bodily passions is neither sensual nor obsessive. They talk without timidity or reserve. The common oaths or exclamations heard in any café or at any street

corner are sexual. Everywhere, people swearing by
their private parts with a Rabelaisian freedom and
laughter. In their speech nothing is hidden. And under
the puritanism of behaviour is something primitive
and animal. It does not occur to them to conceal their
admiration or their desire as they turn in the street to
gaze at the woman who catches their eye; and the
women, who make absolutely no response, nevertheless are very gratified by this admiration. They pity
those women of other countries where public admiration is restrained; they condemn the women of those
countries where such an admiration has an open response. Formal, formal! How often, how many scores
of times during the day, does one hear that almost
military virtue in behaviour exalted! Preserve the
formal, and after that—the whole mystery of private
life, which no one can generalize about.

Chapter VII

When I went to Seville this year in the autumn, I went by train. They turned us all out at Córdoba and packed us into a couple of crowded coaches, and then we clattered along through the milky Andalusian evening. Everyone was entertained by a sparkling, dapper little man of about forty who was travelling with his wife, two nurses, and ten children. The wife, who was pregnant, of course, had a seat, and father hopped about outside, rounding up his chicks every now and then. He was a proud little bantam cock and must have been a man of some means to have such a large family, well fed, well dressed—

and alive. In a poor family so many would not have survived. He was very much admired in the train because that is the sort of family the Spaniards love to see. A shout of delighted laughter went up from many passengers when we got to Seville, for he was met by more women and more children, standing in their midst like a wicked little Abraham, and such a kissing and clucking went on in the swarm that it choked that part of the station. I saw him next day marching a selection of his children round the Cathedral, walking very fast, pointing out works of art, uttering dates and names, in a brisk cultural tour. Then out into the orange courtyard he went and marched them up the ramp of the Giralda for a view of a city—the witty little paternal butterfly.

One comes out into the soft dust of the warm night where the palms droop, into an idle air that smells like no other in Spain. Cool long draughts of aniseed are drawn into the nostrils, the fumes of frying doughnuts. There is no blaze of lights, but the naked electric-light bulbs put their hard, separate tents of light under the palms. Seville is a city of shadows which tunnel under a dense foliage that is dead still, and pleasure seems to walk with one like a person, when one is alone. There is never too much light. In the centre of the small city each street is like a cool narrow channel down which the scents of the jasmine and camellia, of the rose and the orange blossom flow. Once every few years a little snow falls in the winter and excites with wonder the poetic Andalusian, and in the rainy season, before the sun clamps down on the city about Easter, the city can be cold, and few Spanish houses have fireplaces. Even in the coldest cities like Madrid, a room facing south is considered to be heated, and for the rest, there is the *brasero*, with its smouldering charcoal or ground olive stones, which is carried from room to room. But Seville is a town of great heat that stuns the walker, makes him seek the strip of shadow at the side of the wall, or the shade of the courtyard of the orange trees in the Moorish remnant of the Cathedral, or the grottoes and colonnades of the gardens of the Alcázar, where the fountains are sighing and the goldfish rise in hundreds in the jade water of their cisterns. It is a town of pleasure to the eye, where simply to sit or lie down is the deepest of human pleasures, to sit down with nothing in one's head. The spacious Cathedral is the largest Gothic cathedral in the world; it is smaller only than the mosque of Córdoba and St. Peter's in Rome. At every turn one sees the strange, even grotesque mingling of Moorish and Christian art—the tower of the Giralda, visible from so far across the plain, with its severe Moorish mass capped by the florid belfry of the Renaissance; the Alcázar, half Renaissance, half Moorish and even pseudo-Moorish.

The Spanish Temper

These mixtures are bizarre and not always pleasing; one tires of the arabesques, the honeycomb ceilings, the tiled walls and horseshoe arches, especially when they are garish modern imitations, and the Moorish plays the part in Seville (and Granada) of the crudest commercial Gothic in English Victorian architecture. But the great Arab gateways, the heavy, reddened walls, and the tender colours of the true Moorish tiles always please with their gravity and lyricism. The Moors bring a solacing and meditative pleasure into Spanish pomp and glory.

The high moment of Seville is at Easter, when, after a week of the most ornate and pagan processions in Europe, in an atmosphere of theatrical piety and picturesque remorse, the Fair begins and the Andalusian riders in their high hats and leather trouser-facings go by. This is the moment of street parties, pride and ceremony, the supreme moment of display for the women of the city. There is a heavy, torpid beauty. And it is the time of the great bullfights.

Not all the bullrings of Spain are fine. Many of them rise like great red gasworks outside the cities, but the bullring in Seville by the wide slow river is one of the prettiest in Spain. Seville is the city of the bull. The very day when Fernando VII closed the university in Seville, he opened a school for bullfighters there!—a characteristic gesture of Spanish reaction.

Outside the city are the estates where the fighting bulls are bred. In any Spanish town it is common to see boys playing at bullfighting. One sees them waving their shirts at dogs, pretending they are bulls, and the thing to notice is that they are neither playing nor fighting in any violent sense, but going through the stances, the passes, the exhibitions of the national ritual. Outside Seville it is common, at some noisy fair, for someone to shout out: "The bulls!" and for the boys to race down the hill, clamber over the stone walls, and jump down among the bulls to drive them away or to bait them. There is a respect for the bulls. There is admiration of them, but there is no fear, and indeed, in their herds, the bulls are not dangerous. All the same, the Spaniards never lack the courage to make the heroic gesture. The bull is admired, almost worshipped, as the horse is in Ireland. He is admired because he is great and capable of fury, and the Spaniard requires that furious force against which to display his singularity— the most precious of his possessions—and his courage. Always an extremist, he likes to test his courage and his whole personality to the utmost, and he has so contrived the phases of the bullfight that each one has the crisis of decorative perfection that he loves.

Bullfighting is not a sport, and it is therefore not a cruel sport. It is a ritual and a ceremony. It is primitive, barbarous, possibly religious in its remote origin, a descendant of the gladiatorial contest and the mediæval tournament. There are ugly moments in the bullfight, for there are good and bad fights; but since it is conducted in hot blood and in an atmosphere where the swell of great emotion is natural, the killing of the bull is not a sadistic performance; nor does it awaken, I think, cold sadistic emotions in the audience. Their senses are stirred by danger, for the wounding or killing of the bullfighter himself has often occurred. About this one can only say that the Spaniards retain something primitive in their character which was possibly fostered by the *autos de fe* of the Inquisition. Here indeed a terrible and gloating sadism was displayed by the public, sanctified by the Church and approved by the rulers. The Spaniards have strong stomachs. They do not flinch when the blood gushes out of the bull's mouth as he goes down heavily to his death, but in their eyes one sees that proud, frightening brilliance of the conqueror who has emerged from great emotion, who is elated by victory and satisfied by performance. Spanish religious art and the work of Goya reveal a people who do not shy from strong feeling or from the tragedies that fall upon the human body. Above all, they are caught by the drama and the supreme dramatic moment. Undoubtedly they experience the tragic purgation. Undoubtedly there is something savage in it. All historians and the soldiers who have fought against them in the great ages have mentioned the lack of all fear of death in the Spaniards, their stoical indifference to it; all have mentioned the *"furia español."* We know that the Civil War was fought without remorse or quarter, and that indeed the bullrings and vacant lots of the Spanish towns were the scenes of atrocious mass executions. The barbarian is strong in the Spanish people.

The most damaging criticism of the Spanish taste for bullfighting is rather different: the bullfight suffers from the monotony of sacrifices, and it is one more example of the peculiar addiction to the repetitive and monotonous in the Spanish nature. Many foreigners who have known Spain well have noted this taste for monotony. The drama of the bullfight lies within the frame of a foregone conclusion: whatever danger the bullfighter may be in, whatever may be his fate, the fate of the bull is certain. This fact alone removes the bullfight from the complete uncertainty of a sport. It is never certain that the fox will be killed or the boxer knocked out. Inevitably, an English writer is swayed a little by the passionate feeling for animals in England, and will forget the extreme danger to the man. He will forget his bearbaiting and cockfighting past; but even if he does not, and argues that his civilization has come out of that brutal phase, he will fail to notice that although Spain often looks like a modern country,

it is not. The life of Spanish cities runs much closer to
what life was like in England in the seventeenth century; indeed, if one wants to imagine the habits of
London life in the time of Defoe, one cannot do better
than study Madrid or Seville.

Logically the Englishman ought to protest against
the annual casualties in horse-racing and the hunting
field, in a monstrous race like the Grand National,
where fine horses are killed every year. We ought to
see that in the bullfight the danger is to the man. A
number of excellent bullfighters have died in the ring,
for the risk is supreme. In the seventeenth century,
when the bullfight was conducted by the aristocracy
—under more dangerous conditions than are seen today—the Pope tried to stop the fights because of the
great number of deaths. In northern countries, in the
course of the refinement of our civilization, we have
developed a peculiar perversion: better that a man
should be killed than a poor helpless bull! Not all the
hypocrisies are one-sided in this foolish controversy:
the Spaniards grimly reply that they need no Society
for the Prevention of Cruelty to Children in Spain. In
fact, they *have* such societies in the religious orders.
The fatalistic neglect of poor children in the great
cities is hardly touched by charity.

Our final emotion in the bullfight is not with the
bull, which was bred to fight and would, in any case,

have gone to the slaughterhouse, but rests upon the triumphant fighter who has not only pitted his wits against a savage animal and outdone him, but who has done this with the skill, the decorative grace and panache of the artist. It is a male triumph, achieved by courage, art, and obedience to traditional rules.

But the horses? This is a question which has been explained and argued many times since Hemingway became the first Anglo-Saxon apologist of the bull-fight. To most people who are sensitive to spectacle and are capable of pleasure in strong feeling, the sight of these wretched nags blindfolded and weighed down by absurd cushions is grotesque. Before this protection six thousand horses were killed every year. They creak stiffly in like old people, ghastly in their bandaged eyes, repellent in their suggestion of a public hypocrisy. If the bull is killed in hot blood and at the supreme moment of his raging life, the horse is generally injured, and though he might have gone to the knackers the day before, his last moments are ones of terror. For Hemingway, the horse introduced the grotesque note, the necessary element of parody in the spectacle, the counterpoise of low comedy and calamity to the tragic intention of the ritual, for the picador is traditionally an absurd and clumsy fellow, the poor man of the ring. This is an ingenious literary argument; when we consult our reactions at the time

we do not find that they confirm Hemingway's definition. Is it really low comedy such as Shakespeare
pushed into his tragedies to catch the attention of the
low audience? The elegance of the ritual is broken up
by these ghastly buffoons, who are lifted up bodily by
the enormous shoulders of the charging bull. Even
when we are told by sound authorities—and I would
refer the reader to John Marks's excellent book *To
the Bullfight*—that horses are indispensable, for only
a rider has the reach, the strength, and the position for
paralysing the formidable neck muscles of the bull,
and that, until he does that, the man on foot has no
chance of handling the beast—even when we know
this, we squirm at the sight of the pitiful and absurd
cavalcade, which now looks like the man-horse of the
comic circus. And for myself, Hemingway makes the
great error of thinking this comic even in the macabre
sense. It is merely ghastly, a mess; and now that the
horses are cushioned, a cruel and hypocritical mess.
Yet Hemingway has this on his side: the Spanish de-
votees of the bullfight—the *aficionados*—have never
objected to the horses, cushioned or uncushioned: the
mass of Spaniards have a rage for tradition; and the
bullfighting public is "the people" par excellence. The
objections have come from abroad. There is in Spain
a static indifference to animal suffering, or at any rate
a passive, unperturbed regard of it which, after the

primitive barbarities of the Civil War, cannot be denied. In the days of the *autos de fe*, it was the foreign guests at the court who turned their heads from the terrible ceremony in Valladolid and other cities; the Spaniards, either with passions roused or with their customary emptiness of mind, their capacity to experience with their senses, their limited imagination, looked on. I think we must say that the world has not been wrong about the Spaniards: they are, many of them, cruel or undisturbed by cruelty. Either their cruelty is forced up by passion or it is the kind of wayward, unchecked habit of people who have little curiosity, who have long periods of inertia and formlessness in their lives, who do not care to be made to become anything else. A spiritual indolence dwells inside the hard shell of the stoic.

In saying this, one has to recall the very large number of Spaniards who have no taste for the bullfight.

"I went, but I didn't like it," the shopkeeper says.

"Foreigners keep it alive," says the waiter contemptuously.

"I have never been to one. Complete barbarism," says a famous writer.

"Football is killing it," says a football fan.

"Reactionary," says a politician. "It represents everything we have been fighting for generations."

In the last thirty years a puritan opposition to the

bullfight has certainly grown up in Spain. It began with the intellectuals who refused to have anything to do with the fights, and spread especially among the Left-wing groups. The typical Left-wing, anticlerical professor of the Spanish revival in the 1920's and early '30's would say: "The Jesuits told us to go to as many bullfights as we liked, but to avoid the theatre where one picks up dangerous ideas." The liberals and socialists, those engaged in educational, social, and religious reform, thought of the bullfight as the opium of the people.

The bullfight is essentially a passion of the Andalusians, though great bullfights are held in all Spanish cities. In the northern provinces it is less highly regarded. Or rather, there is a form of bull-baiting in the Basque provinces which has no relation to the almost religious ritual of the southern bullfight. Only in the Basque provinces and in Navarre is bullfighting a sport. The most famous, picturesque, and alarming example of it takes place in Pamplona once a year, where the bulls are turned loose in the town and pursue the male population. In the main square of Pamplona the scene is gay, riotous, and terrifying; hundreds of young men are tossed by the bulls, everyone is running, injuries are innumerable. The Navarrese and the Basques are a tough, sporting race, great jousters and acrobats, delighting in physical power and resilience. Between them and the Andalusians, there is not merely that dramatic difference of race which is found in many regions of the peninsula, but the difference between the sportsman and the artist.

The Moors almost certainly brought the bullfight to Andalusia. They held bullfights in the ruins of the Roman coliseum at Mérida, and Moors and Christians competed in the fights. The great Christian hero of Spain, the Cid, is said to have killed a bull, but the first bull was killed by a Spaniard one thousand years ago. By the time of Columbus, the bullfight was an aristocratic tourney. The Emperor Charles V killed his bull. So did Philip IV. The weapon used was the lance, which was presently changed to a short spear. After the decline of its aristocratic phase, the people took over the bullfight and changed it. They fought the bull on foot. The short sword, or *estoque*, now used for killing, came in in 1700, and the *muleta*, the red cape, also. Gradually the present bullfight has evolved its present rigid form. The picador, with his armoured legs and his clumsy peasant air, is the last memory of the nobleman with his lance. Now bull-breeding on the estates in the south is a rich industry, and in the last few years the number of fights has risen to 288 a year. The normal demand for bulls—I quote from John Marks's *To the Bullfight*—"is 3000 three year old bulls and 1500 between four and seven years old,

and the price of a set of six for the corrida is about
£1250." It hardly seems that the bullfight is declining
in its popularity, and, in any case, as far as the rivalry
of football and bullfighting is concerned, the two share
the year between them, for football cannot be played
in the Spanish summer, when the ground is hard and
grassless. But when Hemingway wrote *Death in the
Afternoon* in 1932 and recorded so intimately both
the facts and the gossip of the bullfighters' bars, he
noted that the point of decadence had been reached.
In Manolete—who was killed and has become a kind
of saint to the very emotional following of the bullfight—and in the strange, twisted, intellectual revolutionary, Belmonte, the art (Hemingway thought) had
reached a refinement too great for the spectacle. And
as the art changed, so—or people complain—the bulls
are smaller, faster, but not so furious as they used to
be. In Madrid today one hears that the days of the
great bullfighters are gone.

The ring is packed, silvery with men's suits, black
with women's dresses and then (the only public function in Spain to begin somewhere near time) the great
doors open and the traditional parade of the officers,
the matadors, and their *cuadrillas* (each a team of
seven) steps in brilliant costume across the sanded
arena, followed by the mule team that will drag the
bodies of the dead bulls out of the ring. The president

of the *corrida* throws down the key to the bull pen, the procession leaves, and only three men of the *cuadrilla*, its humblest members, are left in the oval under the sun to receive the first charge of the bull. We have heard him snorting and thumping in his pen and then the gates are opened. Out he comes. He looks either side of the gates, and then, across the arena, he catches sight of the flick of a cape and suddenly gallops towards it. From this moment one's heart is beating hard, one's blood is up. This animal is black, massive, dangerous with a brutal stupidity. The speed of those small legs under the heavy body is remarkable. This first charge of the bull sets the tone of drama; it is a pursuit; the men scurry off, lead him from one to another, and then he viciously decides on his victim and chases him to the stockade. The man vaults over only just in time. I have seen a bull jump the stockade, but there little harm came of it; the crowd bewilders the bull. He is a beast with only one idea at a time.

The bullfight is a play in three acts. First there is the act of the picadors, the horsemen, gross parodies of the mounted noblemen, which is a violent rough-and-tumble. At least nowadays there is no disembowelling. One hears the shock of the bull against the padded horse, and sees the strength of those shoulders that can lift the animal onto its hind legs and perhaps throw the rider. The picador is a much-scarred man, always being pulled from under, and if the bull gets the picador against the stockade the moments are tense, muddled, nasty. The task of the picador is to put his spear into the neck muscles of the bull and paralyse them. The blood spreads like slow paint down its shoulders.

The second act is the moment of the *banderilleros*, the footmen who receive the charge of the bull or buzz about him like dragonflies. They hold a pair of eighteen-inch darts, with paper streamers on them, high above their heads and leap to place them two at a time in the shoulders. And here one has the first sight of the masculine grace of bullfighting, the sight of the male body taut, springing, and accomplished. Four pairs of darts are put into each bull and there they nest and dangle like wasp stings, and yet, also, with a touch of wantonness in their swinging colours.

The fullest account of this, and indeed of all phases of the bullfight, in English, is in Hemingway's *Death in the Afternoon*, and he makes the important point that at no point of the fight is the object to inflict pain on the bull, even though pain is inflicted. The audience is not delighting in cruelty, and, indeed, if you question anyone, you find he is absorbed in the technique of the art. He knows that the darts are there to get the bull's head down and to slow him up until it is possible to kill him. Yet, as Hemingway says, this part of the

189

fight *does* inflict suffering, "some of it useless"; if foreigners admire this part of the fight it is not, however, because they are enjoying cruelty, but because this phase "is easiest to follow."

One pities the stupidity of the animal, and it dawns on one that the bullfight is not a true tragedy, for the forces matched are not of the same kind. It is not a combat between the strength of the man and the strength of the beast, but between the cunning, malice, the art, the will to dominance in the man and the formidable brute stupidity of the beast. Ariel is baiting Caliban, and, in the end, however strong the emotions aroused by the fight, one is eventually bored because the conclusion is foregone (as I said earlier) and because the match is uneven.

And now comes the final act. The matador himself may have planted some of the *banderillas*, and when he does, it is a very pretty act of courage, science, and timing. He knows that once the bull's horns have passed him he is safe, for the animal cannot suddenly turn. And the foreigner, sitting there, becomes aware as he listens to the applause, the abuse, the counterapplause of the crowd, that there is a world of fine points of positioning, approach, and privilege that has escaped him, for the matador is testing himself not only against the bull, but against the experience of the crowd, and the long, long art of tauromachy, which most of them have at their fingertips. The third act of the bullfight is contained in the mystery of the *muleta*, the red cape that conceals the sword, for here lies the matador's chance to play out the famous and beautiful passes when the bull seems to be flicked away by the edge of the cape, or drawn on by its spread or tapering edge, which spins away like a dancer's skirt; and when these passes come quickly one after another in rapid climax, or when they spin out and seem to flower over the back of the charging animal, one hears those unforgettable short, harsh gasps of emotion from the Spanish crowd. All these passes are named: the *veronica*, the natural, the chest pass—there are many, and all aim at some fresh high moment of beauty or danger. They bring out the peculiar character of each matador—perhaps their peasant prudence, the brain of a Belmonte, the grace of a Joselito, the beauty of Manolete, who in their time have been discussed as if they were Velásquezs, Grecos, and Goyas, and not as if they were boxers, wrestlers, or athletes. The literature of bullfighting is written in a language all its own; it has a parallel in the language of art criticism, since the rise of post-impressionist and abstract painting.

The moment of killing is called "the hour of truth," and that is when, over the horns, the sword goes in. The bull stops, stares, totters, then sinks to his knees coughing up his blood and falls dead. The matador salutes the crowd. Hats are thrown in if it is a triumph. Other things if it is not. The Spanish crowd is vocal and nervous. A score of times, as if by a hidden spring, fifty men will rise to their feet in protest, and another fifty near by spring up to challenge them. These protest meetings, suddenly and spontaneously rising and as suddenly fading away, are typical of the bullfight audience, indeed also of audiences at the music halls and theatres. The Spanish protest starts up violently in all things in Spanish life. The bullfighter, the singer, the actor, the dancer, the conductor are, in this sense, the property of the audience, who are extreme in their praise and as sensitive as women to affront. They are the touchiest audiences in the world, careless often of the main setting, regardless of the general atmosphere of human indifference and personal incompetence; but unforgiving and supremely critical of the crisis, the real test, the pass they have waited for. Cynically they sit out the bad bullfights; with vocal despair they watch the bad matador make three or four thrusts and miss. Frequently the sword hits a bone and flies up into the air out of the matador's hand; frequently and unpleasantly it slices the bull's side in clumsy butchery. The hour of truth is often a moment of muddle. Bullfighting is an art, but not all bullfighters are good artists.

The Spanish Temper

In the last twenty years very much has been written about the decadence of the art. The public complains that the bulls are smaller and safer, that they are fought too young, before their terrible horns have spread wide. There are too many small fast bulls, not enough ferocious monsters. I have seen many dull and monotonous bullfights. A foreigner who is not a fan cannot judge these public criticisms. He can only record that many people regard this period as a poor one and, like so many enthusiasts, think the great bullfights took place in their youth. The opinion of Belmonte—whose autobiography, written with the aid of a journalist, is an excellent book, and is likely to have a lasting place among the curiosities of Spanish literature—is worth quoting, for Belmonte revolutionized bullfighting.

The fighting bull of today [he says, writing however in 1937] is a product of civilization, a standardized, industrial article like Coty perfume or Ford cars. The bull is manufactured according to popular demand. . . . The bull is just the same fierce and well-armed wild animal that it was before, but its development has been one-sided toward making the fight more pleasing to the eye. It is not true that it has lost courage. The modern bull charges much more often than the old one, although it is true that it does less damage. I doubt whether one of the bulls which were fought years ago could stand the strenuous *faenas* of today.

193

[*Faena* is the general name for the collection of passes with the cape.]

Belmonte goes on to say that the public wants a bull that is easy to play because they want a fight that "is pretty to see and full of accurate and consistent fancy fighting . . . fancy figures and marvellous patterns." He would have liked to go back to the old tricky, savage, unplayable bulls. Yet when he was fighting the "easy" bulls in 1936, Belmonte fought over thirty *corridas* and was gored fourteen times.

I would not describe Belmonte as a typical matador —if there is such a thing. He was born a slum child in the Triana, the other side of the bridge in Seville, the gypsy quarter, and he picked up his training as an urchin going out into the fields at night and stripping off his shirt to harry the animals in their pasture. It was a form of poaching, and against the law. The urchins often played the bulls naked. Small, stunted by early poverty, often very ill and without great physical strength, Belmonte developed a terrible, almost suicidal intensity, working so close to the bull that after one *corrida* he found his dress covered with the hairs of the animal. He became the intellectual artist of the bullring and was known for years as "the earthquake." He was spiritually rather than physically ambitious. His short, slightly stooping figure with the wide shoulders, the pale face with deep-sunken eyes, and the powerful jaw, which seems to belong to another man, are familiar in the streets of Seville. He has made a lot of money and, with peasant prudence, has saved it, invested it in bull-breeding. His intellectual temperament attracted writers and artists, and Belmonte's passion for excellence, for seeing a disadvantage and making something of it, turned him to education. He was a distinctive figure in that intellectual movement which arose in Spain in the generation before the Civil War and which went to pieces when that war was lost.

The last time I was in Seville I was being pestered by one of those little street arabs who are longing to earn a penny for cleaning your boots, and who, worse still, when you fall for them, begin hammering a rubber sole on them while you read the paper. The first thing I knew about it was a nail going into my foot. After stopping the boy, I asked him his name. He told me and said: "I am Belmonte's secretary."

I thought this was the usual Andalusian joke, and said: "If you are his secretary where does he live?" He pointed to the flat I knew. "And what are your duties?"

"To report first thing in the morning. And to go to school."

"Where is he now?"

"He left his house for his café at eleven. He is going to his farm this afternoon. He will return at seven."

The boy was not making this up. Belmonte *had* taken an interest in the boy, given him odd jobs, appointed him "secretary"—and insisted on his education. The boy was an orphan. Belmonte has the reputation of one who prudently watches his money—Hemingway has stories of this—and in this shows himself a true, pretty tightfisted Andalusian; but his admiration for intelligence and determination, which the boy had, must have made him think of his own half-starved childhood. Belmonte's insistence on schooling is typical. When he first went to France, as an ignorant young man, he did not come back repelled and chauvinistic about French civilization as many Spaniards do; on the contrary, he was quick like all the best of his generation to see the superior ease and refinement of European life.

The crickets sing under the palms of the squares of Seville, the barrel organs roll out their *flamenco* music, the shrines are lighted like little dolls' houses in the narrow streets, there is the smell of jasmine, broken by the reek of oil or the frying of prawns. Artisans at their trades easily break into song in all Spanish towns. The cobbler hammers away alone, singing out:

The Spanish Temper

"Today is Saturday, Today is Saturday!"

as if that line were a poem in itself. At night the crickets are shriller and louder; one small insect will be heard across the square. In the Barrio Santa Cruz, where each street bears its name in large, simple black letters that have been there since the seventeenth century, one seems to be walking on cobbled porcelain, and by the weak yellow light of the tiled courtyards, one sees the gloss of the evergreens and the ferns, the hard leaves of the orange tree, and hears the gurgle of a small fountain. Darkness, jasmine, water, and white walls. One passes the sedate small baroque churches, which are like the ornate little drawing-rooms of God, and there one may see the pearled Virgins or the carved Christs that are borne by the brotherhoods in the processions of Holy Week. Again, the continuous play of contrast in Spanish life strikes the traveller. The plain, frugal, simple life matched by the passion for some crystallization of ornament or decoration. The plain wall has the superb encrusted carving; the massive door, the wrought-iron gate, opens from the sun's glare in the street upon a darkness that, as the eye becomes accustomed to it, gradually begins to glitter with the fierce brilliance of gold leaf and rococo. It is a greed, but carried to the pitch of extravagant art.

197

And as one listens to the rapid, whirling, laughing music of the Sevillana, as hard as perpetual gaiety, as grave as coquetry, as one listens to the talking, rhythmic crackle of castanets, one has in mind also the cockroaches on Mañara's velvet, the sombre steps of the barefooted and black-cowled penitents of the processions, the bitter scream of the *saetas* sung in the silence when the procession stops and the sweating bearers put down their loaded images for a rest. So strange are Spanish religion and love: in the eighteenth century, penitents used to scourge themselves in the street with a cat-o'-nine-tails that terminated in small balls of wax and glass, and especially paused in front of their ladies to lash harder and gratified these adored ones by splashing them with their blood. Blood, sensuality, death—Maurice Barrès was not altogether wrong about the Spanish voluptuary. If voluptuousness is the word.

One sits at the café table watching the crowd go by. There are no mass men; each one is acting out a distinctive role. One sees a variety of feature, as large as anything in Gilray or Rowlandson, from the emaciated beggar, the exalted blind, to the young dandy wagging his buttocks, the bullfighter and his court, and the sad gluttons of the city. There goes the gambling Marquis looking satanically the part, and his toady, the young doctor living under his mother's thumb. There the doctor stands talking to one of his many illegitimate gypsy children, who sells him a lottery ticket. In the upper room of some house, a succulently fat young man, "ruining himself with a woman," may be seen lolling with the fat young creature, who has already two soft chins, with friends in attendance. Socially the *sevillanos* hold court and are not solitary in their pleasures. No engagement books, no telephone numbers, no addresses—you seek your friend in the street, you whistle up the first urchin you see and send him with the message. No hours are kept. "Well," how often one overhears the remark, "we shall see each other when we see each other, if not, not, but here or there, sometime." Find the man in his café, or in his barber's, or in the other café. One pursues him round the town. At his house— he has always "just gone out." The home—that is the closed place. If he is there, that is the end of his social life for that day. Outside, any time up to two or three in the morning you will find him. Life is the street. They are not shut away as we are. They have few secrets. They are at ease publicly in their virtues and vices, and their habits. Unamuno again: "Nothing human is alien to me." A foreigner becomes bored, in the end, by the plain explicitness of Spanish life and of seeing so many basic and unabashed human beings who conceal nothing; but, for a time, the Spaniard, not seriously touched by the industrial age or the nervousness of modern man, is powerfully refreshing. He is a man before he is a specialist, a unit, a function of the social machine. Only when we consider him as a social being are we appalled by his intolerance, his cruel inertia, and, in Seville, by the coarseness of his boasting. There is a street in Seville now named after the Falangist hero of that city, Queipo de Llano, whose rollicking, boasting, and blood-thirsty broadcasts were famous in the Spanish Civil War. Yet a drunken picaresque spirit, as outrageous as the picaresque in *Don Juan*, loud and raking, belongs to the place. The *sevillano* is stingy; but he is an actor; he loves the idea of great and notorious sins of the flesh. So many of the *sevillanos* have the coarse skins of those oranges that fall at last to rot in the alleys of the beautiful park, and from their faces the old Silenus looks out of wine-reddened eyes. But fiercely they will maintain the punctilio of God, the sacredness of the family, the world-breaking greatness of the country, and the wicked irreligion of the working class.

Chapter VIII

The hotels are packed out in Granada, in the spring and the autumn. They have always been full in the last two years since the exchange has been made advantageous to foreigners. These are mainly French. There are a few British and a great many Americans. Lately, those old Spanish enthusiasts, the Germans and Swiss, have started to come again. We are all regarded as ridiculous by the Spaniards who are helpful, polite, dry, and never obtrusive. It is better to be high up in Granada, on the cliff of the Alhambra, though now there is an excellent hotel in the lower part of the town, but the lower part is noisy and very ugly. The main street is a prosperous nineteenth-century Oxford Street, though it has not yet been cursed by the multiple store. The retail trade remains firmly Victorian.

The people of Granada, it must be confessed, have a proud, stiff, superior, and unsmiling appearance, which is exceptional in the south, and are more Castilian than Andalusian. One sees many Moorish types. The *granadinos* have a reputation for conceit and avarice, and they are certainly more self-enclosed than the effusive *sevillanos*, whom they despise for their play-acting and boasting. For a hundred years there has been social and political tension in Granada, controlled on the surface, rabid underneath. Many years ago I used to go and see Don Fernando de los Ríos, one of the socialist leaders of the province, and a professor at the university. He was a connection of Francisco Giner de los Ríos, the great educational reformer and saint of that excellent minority of intellectuals who had become followers of Kraussism—an extinct German philosophy. Fernando de los Ríos was eminent in the Republic, but wisely worked outside of Spain in the Civil War; for by nature all his group, the one group which might have done something for Spain, despaired of the extremism of both sides. I had many lectures on the land problem in Spain from Don Fernando, many decorous and exhaustively cultural visits to the hidden architectural beauties of Granada. He was known everywhere, especially in the Albaicín, the old Moorish quarter, and would take one into delightful carmens, or villas, and to modest houses where one would find a horseshoe arch of the Moors in a bedroom or a few delicate Moorish tiles, so graceful after the hideous, restored or newly manufactured tiles of the Alhambra.

Don Fernando was a respectable man. He was a little stout, sometimes wore a frock coat, but always a black coat, and pinstripe trousers. He had a fine black beard and a soft, educated, and persuasive voice, and a gentle enunciation.

"Look," he would say, pointing to a book on a student's bookcase, and speaking with that curious religious glee one often hears in the voice of some precious, finger-wagging priest. "Look—he has his *Das Kapital*."

And Don Fernando would regard the little volume of economic dynamite with the childish affection a scientist will show for a new bomb. Don Fernando thought of revolution poetically, and with a certain unworldly pomposity. He had, of course, been in prison as a politician at one time in his life, and his loftiness and immaculate gravity caused a good deal of that picaresque malice which the Spanish tongue cannot repress, especially when it concerns their closest friends. It was fitting that Don Fernando eventually ascended to the eminence of an embassy.

Don Fernando was not suited to Spanish political life; very few of the admirable Spanish intellectuals were. Their true function was to teach and to conduct the bitter struggle for educational reform against the opposition of the Jesuits. Once in politics, Don Fernando became a fanatic. But as a humane and enlightened man he was regarded with respect and awe in Granada, and is remembered proudly now as a figure of the excellent and defeated generation. Spanish liberalism does not die out. It is merely silenced.

I have drawn his portrait in order to indicate the character of social and political life in Granada. In spite of his eminence or his notoriety there, he was isolated in the life of that very rich, very snobbish and conservative city. He and his family were cut off from the social life of the town. The Spaniards have a sort of caste snobbery unmatched in Europe, and the perennial calamity of their political and religious differences is that they shut their doors on their opponents. It is not "done" to read much, think much, or act much, outside the direction of the governing class—whatever it is—or the Church. Partly, Spanish family pride is at the bottom of this; partly, it is the old, old influence of absolutism. One has to remember that the Inquisition lasted until 1834 and put its stamp on what was correct. For ideological good behaviour becomes social good behaviour; it creates the socially "right" people and the "wrong."

Granada was the city of García Lorca, who was assassinated during the Civil War in one of the savage reprisals of the time. He has been criticized for remaining in a city so hostile, but it is known for its poets, like many Andalusian towns, and all Spaniards are profoundly attached to their birthplace and their region. A *granadino* remains a *granadino* for ever. Granada fell as quickly as Seville to General Franco at the beginning of the Civil War, and executions are said to have disposed of twenty thousand people. Nine thousand were "officially" shot—that is to say, an official list of their names exists. One of these was García Lorca. The whole of Andalusia was a stronghold of the anarchist movement, which swept Andalusia like a religious revival in the last quarter of the nineteenth century. This region of slave labourers had quickly turned to the millennial doctrine of anarchism, and especially to the religious idea that all wealth was wicked. The anarchists did not wish to become as rich as the middle classes, for they thought of them as corrupted by even small private wealth. They perhaps *were* corrupted, but in a sense the anarchists do not mean: the Spanish middle classes have never been rich enough and they have been obliged to keep their hands sharply on their small incomes. Like the anarchists, the middle classes have been self-mutilated by the obsession with the idea of a minimum.

Anarchism must not be confused with anarcho-syndicalism, which sought to organize the workers as a revolutionary force, and whose weapon was the violent general strike. Whereas the Communists wanted the state to control everything, the anarcho-syndicalists wanted final control to be exercised by the trade unions. Sorel, the philosopher poet of anarcho-syndicalism, with his mystique of violence, was little known in Spain. The Spaniards provided a mystique of violence spontaneously. Anarcho-syndicalism was Red (but, of course, savagely anti-Communist), and, in fact, its ideas resembled closely those of the Falange or the national syndicalism theoretically in operation under Franco's regime in Spain today. Both brands, the Left and the Right, have been murderous: the reason lies in the native violence of the people who provided Goya with his horrors one hundred and fifty years ago, and in the condition of the country.

Anarchism is especially the doctrine of the thousands of poor casual labourers or serfs called in to work on large estates in dry and unfertile country. Anarchism does not exist where the peasants own the land. But in Granada there is a complication. I stood among the lilies and cypresses and roses of the beautiful gardens of the Generalife, watching one of those prolonged crimson sunsets which are the supreme sight of Granada, and asked the professor of Arabic what he supposed the Moors talked about as they sat in the *mirador* looking over the plains to the miles of sharptoothed, violet mountains.

"Politics," he said. "Always politics. A little love, a little poetry—but mostly politics. We know it. It is in the documents. It is the great Spanish evil. We are supposed not to talk politics today—but we do. It is like breathing."

And the politics of Granada spring from the warm wealth of its plain and those narrow fertile valleys that reach out to the caves, the desert and moon landscape of Murcia and Almería to the east and south, and tenuously link it with the rich dark green oases that lie beyond.

The *vega* or plain of Granada, and the smaller *vega* of Murcia (Brenan points out in *The Spanish Labyrinth*), are the only irrigated districts of Spain which are not in the hands of small proprietors. Large fortunes have been made out of crops like sugar beet, and rents are enormously high. The social conflict has been bitter, for the ordinary labourer is not a serf here, but a man one or two rungs up the ladder of social education; he used to be a well-trained socialist or radical in politics who knew how to organize and negotiate. The landowners were on the extreme Right, but there were notable exceptions: there was not complete solidarity between the few small and the many large landowners. A moderate property makes a man liberal; a large property turns him into a despot. Socialism itself, where it has organized large collectives, has been despotic.

There is now reviving prosperity in the south, a small revival. I went about with a lawyer, a man going on for forty, who was in the usual situation of a Spaniard of the middle class: he practised as a solicitor part of the day, he taught in a school, and he was a "crammer" in mathematics in the evening. His wife was a schoolmistress. Each had to earn in order to survive, and since Granada was, he said, "stagnant" as far as the law was concerned, he was trying to set up in Madrid. One has learned to see that anxious, hard look in the faces of those Spanish middle-class people who are industrious. In every Spanish town one comes across these energetic men who loathe the provincial towns, and are like the doomed characters in a Chekhov story. One meets them in Pío Baroja's novels. It is a fundamental Spanish theme: how to get out, and especially if one is a man of some education and with a taste for what other Spaniards contemptuously call "the European." The pay of schoolteachers is wretched, but Granada has one or two open-air schools, run on something like the Dalton plan. They survive from the period of educational revival in the first thirty years of the century; under the present regime they are confronted by the fanatical syndicalist schools of the Falange, where the main theme is a diluted form of fascist indoctrination. How deep does fascism go, how forceful is it? Always the answer, from the ordinary person outside the movement, is that while still occasionally tiresome, dogmatic, and threatening, it has lost a great deal of its edge. The "eternal Spain," indefinable because so various, so atomized by regional differences, is indolently nullifying it. It survives not only because it alone has the power, but because, exhausted and appalled by the war, Spaniards are politically bewildered and self-mistrustful.

The tourists are dumped in the hotels on the cliff where the Alhambra and the summer palace of the Generalife stand, and watch through air as crystalline as mountain water, the theatrical southern sunset. The lights spring up, clear and single, thousands of them, from the little houses of the immense plain. The air is soft and the nights are cool. Granada lies under the snow of the Sierra Nevada and can be icy cold. The smoke of lavender and gorse, the fume of charcoal, rise from the roofs of the town below, where the people are fanning their stoves, where the strong oil fries. All windows are open and only one weak naked bulb lights the rooms. One needs a strong stomach for Spanish travel, and sooner or later one is bound to go down with diarrhœa or mild poisoning; I do not believe this is due to the water, for I have drunk it without ill effect in most places. It must be said, however, that the water of Granada has not lately had a good reputation. If one has survived the heavy meal that night, one will be carried to see the gypsies dance at one of the big hotels or in their caves. It is a curious fact that the best dancers go to the hotels, for in other countries the hotels have had a corrupting influence on local talent. The Spanish hotels have, in fact, not spoiled the dancers, and exercise a sound authority on them. The proprietors are critical; in the caves, though one crouches in the firelight or smoke, the atmosphere is more "typical" and picturesque, but the dancing sometimes ragged, exaggerated, and merely violent. The gypsies are, artistically, very corruptible, though they have their dances in their bones. They especially like to give one a display of dishevelled, animal fury, in which they whirl like typhoons, claw their hair, and contort themselves like wildcats, and in this they indeed show their mastery of the savage possibilities of the dance; but it is in their controlled verve, their capacity to convey the gradual crescendo of passion, the tightening of the nerves, the sense of sexual battle and the human being possessed by desire and reaching the utmost pitch of it before attack or surrender, that their art is direct and certain. It is the calculated, stylized advance towards orgy which these supple bodies best convey. The Roman poet Martial, who was born in Spain, wrote nearly two thousand years ago of the sensual power and fury of the Spanish dancers. Their comic or satirical dances soon drift into raucous vulgarity. Bullfighters, singers, dancers come out of the smart caves of the Granada hillside. Many of the gypsy families are rich. In the Albaicín, the old site of the Moorish quarter, there are many gypsies who have got on in the world and gone into the professions. I met one and, unlike the typical member of the despised races, he told me straight out at the point of introduction: "I am an educated gypsy. I am a doctor. In my generation a large number of us left the caves and have greatly improved our status"—he spoke in this formal way.

The cave-dwellers of Granada are the most prosperous troglodytes in Spain. There are many others. Outside Guadix, on the road to Murcia, is another more striking colony, for here the treeless landscape of the igloo-like boulder and serrated rock gives an oddity to their appearance. Near Vera, a wretched town of

Murcia, there is the large village of Cuevas. Three thousand people live outside this town in caves cut into the cliffs.

To the northerner, emerging from his air-raid shelter, the caves of Granada and the Murcian region are a horror. The cave-dwellers themselves find the curiosity of the foreigner very amusing. In these climates where rainfall is small, the cave is dry and cool in the summer, warm in the winter. The rudimentary cave—where an old man lives alone with his few goats—is of three rooms cut into the earth—one to sleep in, one to live in, the other one for the animals. But most caves are handsomer than this. In Granada they are whitewashed, well furnished with good solid furniture. Pictures are on the wall—the oleographs of saints and nineteenth-century generals which are in all the houses of the Spanish poor—the tiled stove shines, and the smoke comes out of a chimney on the surface of the ground above among the cactus. There is usually electric light. Sanitation does not exist, but that is true of the outskirts of many Spanish towns. The church wall, the back alleys, and the walls of some old castle are the latrines of the shanty-dwellers. Oil, urine, excrement, tobacco, and the smoke of lavender wood—those are the savours of the outlying districts of Spain; indeed, not only of the outlying ones.

The Spanish Temper

At Cuevas one brilliant gypsy mother with her grown-up children showed me round with pride. The floor was tiled, the sideboard and the large double bed in walnut indicated some standing and property. Her daughter—this being late in the afternoon—had her hair well done and a pretty frock on, like a girl from the city. She might have been a genteel typist. Her eldest son, with his gold tooth or two, his good suit and plump figure, was prosperity itself; he walked about carrying a baby on his arm, and holding a dove on his finger.

"Say '*ocho*' " (eight), he told them all when I took a photograph, "to make you smile."

He had a good job as a barber to a monastery. The dwellings at Cuevas are cut in the red wall of the hillside, their entrances marked by outlines of whitewash. Some were poor and people were cooking outside. They were all casual labourers here, sitting in the sun half the year waiting to be called to the round of crops. The fine straw dust of the esparto grass was their curse; it had ruined the eyes of many. They were not all gypsies, and they had the easy dignity and good manners of an aristocracy.

The climb up the steep hill out of the ugly town of Granada towards the Alhambra is a climb for air and respite from the noise in which Spaniards love to live. The morning sun is beginning to sting with its flame-

like lick, the bones are softening. One moves towards
the foot of shade by the dusty wall. The sun beats
like some brassy enemy, and in the cold winters of
Granada one notices the sudden ice shock of Spanish
shade when one steps out of the sun into it; there are
always, winter or summer, these two violently different climates of sun and shade, as if there cannot be
a mean or gradualness even in the simple step one takes
along the road. We must be either hot or cold. The
gooseflesh of Spanish religious painting comes, perhaps, not from a mortification of the body, but from
that starving coldness which is everywhere waiting,
suddenly to grip the whole body in Spain, when the
sun has unclasped it, the ice cold of the cloister, the
patio, the room in the inn.

Charabancs, motorists, walkers, all climb to the
Alhambra, the expected marvel, rising into the profound shadow of the woods where one seems to be
treading on the music of water which races down
through the trees, and where at night the nightingales
sing. The bizarre traits of Victorian tourism appear at
the approaches; the Alhambra would not be the same
without them now. The tourist is part of the landscape
of our civilization, as the pilgrim was in the Middle
Ages. There are still those photographers where the
grinning foreigner straightens his face and, dressed up
in Moorish robes, is "taken" against a confected Moor-

ish arch and a little tracery—betrayed by the un-Moor-
ish plumpness of his cheeks and the absurd, alien expressiveness of his eyes. A naïve prosperity and the
terrible tameness of industrial man on holiday betray
these innocent parodies; they have felt, what all must
feel in the Alhambra, a pathetic desire to get rid of
everybody and to slide five hundred years back into
that time.

Except for its massive and splendid outer walls and
gates, which are the main beauty of the place, the
Alhambra is a gay and flimsy construction. Above the
arcading of the marble pillars of its courtyards, the
construction is of lath and plaster; the place itself recalls a collection of pretty exhibition buildings which
have not worn well with time and have been continually restored. Workmen are always restoring some
part of the palace, and the output of Moorish tiles and
filigree amounts to one of Granada's notable industries.
The colours are now hard and garish, as we now see
them, and, for myself, the only interest is in the stalac-
tite ceilings. They hang, like wasps nests, from the
roofs, but what they immediately suggest is the pano-
ply or the tent, and indeed the greater tent of the sky.
One is looking up with the eyes of the Arab astrono-
mers at a stereoscopic vision of the night sky, the peaks
of the stars, and the suspended valleys of space. These
ceilings are the voluptuous dreams of mathematicians,

a sensuous yet pedantic interweaving of the patterns of space. For the rest, the Alhambra is a site. Its delight lies in its windows that look into the cypresses of some small courtyard where a single fountain plays and the roses are fragrant, or out into space upon the clear air of the wide, gasping views towards the snow on the Sierra Nevada, or the terracotta roofs of the old Moorish quarter below, the Albaicín—which is the only agreeable part of the town. A good wine can be drunk there in one or two of the bars, but like the best things in Spain it is a local wine coming from one vineyard. I doubt if it is known outside one or two places in the long descending street where the market of the Albaicín is spread out on the cobbles or the doorsteps. The wine is called La Costa; it is a little like a dry port, and it is fortifying in the heat.

Water and shade, air like spring water to breathe: these are the true delights of the Alhambra. As a piece of architecture it cannot compare with the great mosque at Córdoba. But, craftsmen and pedants in everything, the Moors of Granada knew how to work for small delights. The richness of the *vega* protected by its violet mountains lying back in the heat by day and coming forward, sharp as knives, when the sun goes down; the sunlight and the abundance, civilized the men from Africa and softened them. Dazed, indifferent, they let the Spaniards live. They intermarried, and when Fernando the Catholic conquered them, after his ten years' siege ("taking," as he is supposed to have said, "this pomegranate seed by seed"), he was really conquering a race who had become Spaniards by six hundred years of adoption. Hence the violence of the forcible conversions, the repressions that caused the rising in the Albaicín and the massacre that followed: the King was imposing the Faith upon those who ought to have it. He had guaranteed religious freedom to the defeated Moors, which for centuries they had allowed the Christian; but, seven years after the conquest, the Church, in the person of Cardinal Ximénes, obliged the people to burn all their Arabic books. Nor was forcible conversion enough for Spanish extremism and intolerance. The *moriscos*, once converted, were at once suspected of false conversion. Their use of water, so detested by the Christians, was often enough to incriminate them in the eyes of the Inquisition. Nor were these purges satisfactory to the first totalitarians of Europe. In the first decade of the seventeenth century the *moriscos* of Spain were deported, as the Jews had been before them. Their skills, their labour went with them; and a rich country was left in the hands of people more concerned with guerrilla warfare and the idle, soldierly, and frugal satisfaction of their wants. Useless for landlords to try and prevent the loss of their valuable workers: Spain was always willing to sacrifice reality to an idea.

The Moorish occupation was long, and it can be said that Spain civilized the men of the desert who brought their own bloody quarrels with them. Their heights of civilization were achieved only after long periods of fighting, as each new wave came over the straits into the Promised Land. The Spaniards, divided from one another in the regions like different nations, frequently fought for the Moors against their own kind. The traditional Spanish hero, the Cid, fought for the Arabs against them, and he was less a knight of Christian chivalry than a soldier of fortune.

In his *History of Iberian Civilization* the Portuguese historian Oliveira Martins tells us that at the peak of their civilization, between the eighth and thirteenth centuries, the Arabs had more than seventy libraries at Córdoba, Málaga, Almería, and Murcia, and that they were the masters, doctors, and soothsayers of the Christian kings, just as the Jews were their financiers and bankers. But Arab culture was that of artists rather than thinkers; "setting store almost exclusively by imagination and scarcely employing reason . . . they gave the preference to beautiful forms, elegant style or subtlety . . . their love of Greek science was a mere caprice, not a need of the spirit." In Almería, that hot little Oriental town hemmed in by rock against the sea, on the road going eastward from Málaga, where the splendid Arab castle is cut out like a golden crown above the little city which had, centuries before, been one of the richest towns in Spain and the Western World—in Almería the nobility and the kings, "sceptical in religion and indifferent in politics, gave themselves up to a life of childish literature," composing exquisite little lyrics and madrigals of love. No vestiges of the Arab rule, Oliveira Martins says, remained in the civil institutions of the people of the peninsula, owing to the toleration of the Arabs, the difference of religion, and the artificial character of Arab culture. The real influence of the Arab conquest is to be seen in the direction it gave to the national life of modern Spain. Born in the camp in the midst of battle, the character of Spain springs rather from spontaneous sources than from the ordinances of ancient tradition, Roman or Germanic.

To the east of Granada lies the province of Murcia, and to the south-east is Almería. The last consists of wide stretches, miles and miles of them, of depopulated country. The region is one of painful and dilatory train journeys that wind away from their destination towards distant junctions and then coil back. All journeys take all day. Once outside of big cities like Barcelona, Madrid, Valencia, and Seville, once one is lost somewhere in the provinces, one is generally obliged to be awakened at three or four in the morning in order to catch the *rápido*. That night scene in the commercial *fonda* of small Spanish towns is always terrible and inevitable. The station will lie two miles outside the town, a shattered old brake will meet the trains. The night porter, who has been coughing and spitting half the night at the door, goes round banging and shouting at the bedroom doors, waking up the wretched passengers. If one happens sleepily to wander into the kitchen by mistake, one will see perhaps a cook or two lying fast asleep on the kitchen table, and wearing those peculiar white calico combinations tied with tape at the ankles, while the maid sleeps on some bedding at the bottom of a cupboard. Spanish sleeping is always crowded. At the junction for Plasencia in Extremadura many years ago, I saw two men carrying an iron bedstead into the ticket office. They put the bed together and presently the enormous stationmaster, with a great deal of gold braid on him, slept there in blue and white striped pyjamas which heaved like a marquee under his snores. He was waiting for the sublime moment of his life: the arrival of the night train. This region can be crossed by the local buses, which are always packed with live-stock and human beings, but life in the small villages will try the stomach of the traveller.

Leaving Granada, the road climbs and falls into the

narrow rich valleys that lie between the city and the dry yellow town of Guadix, and though Guadix has its poplars and eucalyptus trees, its maize and its vines, it is on the edge of the desert. The Cathedral dominates the town like a wily old southern landlord, fat, dawdling, and pock-marked. It contains some of Churriguerra's fantastic ornamentation, that sculpture of emblazoned tripes; it corresponds to the element of ornate presumption and worldly fantasy which is one aspect of the Spanish taste for excess. It is a good thing to indulge this taste by a journey northwards to the town of Lorca, a high place of some rather destitute elegance which is rich in creations of the eighteenth century, and where Churriguerra may be enjoyed in the eight churches of the town. The doorway to the palace of the Guevara family and the enormous staircase within are worth seeing.

But this is a digression from Guadix, where some cave-dweller, hoping for an American cigarette—for they do not value their own pure black tobacco—is asking one to visit the caves. I have already described these caves. The interest of those at Guadix is their bizarre setting opposite the town. One might be looking at the rock islands of the Mexican or Arizona landscape. One is looking at what appears to be a collection of bowler hats made out of rock, or rather of peculiar kettles, for each one has a chimney striking out of the top of it. Each hat or kettle contains a number of caves. On a Sunday here one notices that although the children may be half-naked—which is sensible in the sun—the young women are well dressed. The "good appearance" is a law. At Guadix the cave-dwellers have been visited by so many motorists now that they are vain of themselves as a curiosity, but they do not molest as much as Italian peasants and children; dignity and self-containment, the restful and smiling indifference of the Spaniards, are their protection. Like the rest of their nation they regard the foreigner as fantastic, abnormal, absurd, a person of the wrong religion and intolerable ideas. Envy and covetousness do not exist. They are shocked by the sight of wealth and the kind of work we have to do in order to get it. The general attitude of the Spaniard, from the cave-dweller to the grandee, to those who point out the beauties of social reform, better health and housing, is possibly polite agreement, but it is generally angry resentment; fundamentally, the attitude is that it is we who live in a spiritual slum which the Spaniards could rescue us from, if they felt the effort worth while—but they do not. In a few years we shall have blown ourselves to pieces or killed ourselves off by a germ warfare, and the survivors will then see the irresistible but unattainable advantage of the Spanish way of life.

The Spanish Temper

At Guadix one looks out upon one of those pano-
ramas of rock and mountain which are the delight of
the peninsula. It is a land for the connoisseur of landscape, for in no other European country is there such
variety and originality. Here Nature has had vast
space, stupendous means, and no restraint of fancy.
One might pass a lifetime gazing at the architecture of
rock and its strange colouring, especially the colouring of iron, blue steel, violet and ochreous ores, metallic purples, and all the burned, vegetable pigments.
These landscapes frighten by their scale and by the
suggestion of furrowed age, geological madness, ma-
levolence, and grandeur. One is looking out on a perspective of causeways, going up step by step, for
miles at a time to the steeper walls of the horizon, and
each step worn into short vertical furrows. The colours are gold, brown, violet, slate by turns, the
aspect that of a wrinkled face, the scale gigantic. One
is entering upon those mountains that seem like the
coarse, plated hides of the rhinoceros. The sight ap-
pals. Once pine forests were here, but now the only
pines one sees are a few "trees," no more than a foot
high, planted in the stones of the roadside. Rain is a
mere memory. Worse appears if one goes down to
Almería by way of Vera. These lumpish mountains
open at one point into an enormous amphitheatre,
twenty or thirty miles across, perhaps more. Range

after range surrounds it until the farthest are a faint ring of tossing flames. One can only say that Nature has died and that merely its spectre, geology, remains. It is simply chaos. Ravines are gashed out, sudden pinnacles of rock shoot up five hundred feet into the air; their tops seem to have been twisted by whirlwind, the Ice Age has eaten into their sides, the Great Flood has broken their splitting foundations into gullies. This amphitheatre is the abandoned home of fire and water, for only wind lives there now; the colours are of the rusted knife, the bruised body, the bleached bone. For miles the road follows a watercourse which lies in a deep and ragged ravine, but it is simply a shingle bed with no water in it. There has not been water for years. It is rare to see a human being; and if one does, it will be a man making a fire in the bed, burning, I suppose, the soda plant. Or one will pass the solitary lime-burner.

But an oasis begins after one has dropped over the mountains into the outskirts of Almería. Almería is a hot little seaport cooped into a hole below the coastal range. It has doubled its population since the middle of the last century and has a rich trade abroad with the small Almería grapes, figs, and esparto grass. There is some air of prosperity. The town lies in its heat like a plum soaked in brandy. The thermometer never goes below 60° Fahrenheit in the winter, but it can go up to nearly one hundred in the summer. It is hard to think of Almería now as "the Manchester of Spain"; it was really a counterpart of Algiers, a "pirates' nest," and in the time of the Moors—it was conquered a few years before Granada—it was considered greater than Granada, which was called the mere inland granary or farm of the seaport. The Cathedral at Almería looks like a fortress, and was indeed one: it was built to repel the attacks of pirates.

I listened one hot afternoon to the priests droning out their Latin there in their powerful, wonderfully snarling resonant southern voices that establish the authority of the classical tongue by incantation, its hypnotizing and inescapable sense of order, its degeneration into a sort of monotonous groaning of the prayer wheel. The sound puts a spell upon the listener, its rhythms suggest the sessions and durbars of Ashanti, creating the spell of communal rule. To what noise in contemporary life can one compare this endless chanting, which goes on in a vacuum; to the hum of a factory? To the monotonous propaganda poured out on the radio, which no one listens to, not even God? The superiority of the Roman incantation, mechanical, unheeding, torpid, is manifest, and the Spaniards settle to it with all the ease of habit. It is always pleasant to watch a choir or to see people self-enchanted. It was a hot afternoon; in the pauses, these large, fat, impor-

tant men yawned, scratched an itching leg, and got
through the dawdling routine of the religious vocation.
The Spanish priesthood are casual in their devotions
and treat ceremony lazily, like a donkey taking them
to market; the magic is an everyday affair, and in Spain
one feels that is how it should be. I ought to say I have
heard brisker performances by men in Castile and indeed was once shown the El Grecos at Illescas by one
Sister in white who left her choir and came round
singing with me from picture to picture, with sweet-
ness and propriety.

The light that flashes off the Mediterranean is intolerable to the eyes in the morning at Almería. The
English used to come out this way from Gibraltar in
the nineteenth century, before Málaga became fashionable, and the best hotel in the town has the English
Victorian spaciousness and disorder. Its galleries, its
pictures, its knotty armchairs have Victorian charm.
There are two excellent restaurants in the main street:
shellfish, the langouste and langoustine, and mayon-
naise and white wine are brought.

The mountains rise steeply out of the town itself.
From the top of the Moorish castle one looks down on
a flat-roofed city which is Oriental in its greater part;
down below the red-wheeled horse-cabs trot. The
main street is shaded by the low thick branches of the
fristo trees, and under them half the population seems

to sit all day and half the night. By day, they sit like flies drowned in syrup, unable to move because of the weight of the sun, unable, almost, to talk. When they do talk, their minds run easily to conceits which, as we have read, also preoccupied the Arab courts.

"Why are there so many police in this town?" I asked a man who was sitting at my table, for I could count nearly twenty in various uniforms within a hundred yards. He turned his head slowly and as slowly turned it back again.

"There are not many police," he said.

Then a conceit occurred to him; he glittered for a moment in the southern way.

"When you see policemen in the main street, it is because a policeman lives for his uniform. He wants it to be admired. They gather here to enjoy their uniforms. The middle of a town is the policeman's mirror." This fancy exhausted him.

"Nothing," he said. *"Nada."* Or *"Nichevo."* The end of a southern conversation: a sudden whizzing journey up to the sky like a rocket, a burst, and then extinction, nothing.

There was a lame lawyer—and Spain is full of anxious, idle lawyers; half the students take law at the universities—standing in the doorway of a postcard shop. A man of forty. He started in a pious, caressing voice to say how he would like to kiss General

Franco's feet for the blessings he had brought. This lawyer had read a great deal, chiefly poetry and the novels of Camus and Sartre: he loathed them for their realism.

"There is going to be a great romantic revival," he cried out in an exalted, pretty way. "The world is becoming romantic. Pessimism is going. There is joy. Everywhere," he said. "In the heart," and he plucked at his breast. "In the spirit," he said, boring a delicate finger into his ribs. "In the mind," he said, pinching his eyebrows together with four fingers.

"After twenty years of horror?" I said.

"Because of them. I will give you an example. In the Civil War I was arrested by the Reds and I was put into prison. I was condemned to death. I saw my friends, some of the good people in this town, taken off to be shot. Good—well! I went last year back to the place where we were imprisoned. I went to the very room, the very corner where I used to be. It wasn't horrible. It was marvellous. 'Here,' I said, 'is where I lay. Here So-and-so died beside me, and from here many were taken out and seen no more.' And I was happy. I was not sad. I wasn't happy because I had escaped, but because I lived it all again. I felt ecstasy. That is what the world is feeling now, ecstasy at having lived through these terrible times—exultation, a heroic feeling that one has been chosen. It is romantic. It is poetic. It is strange. It is not like the realism of Cela [a very good young novelist in Madrid] or Sartre."

A bootblack in the same town who had been a refugee on the road from Málaga when it was bombarded had been, unlike the lawyer, a Red. He said very much the same thing: the horrors were unspeakable, but "the sensation of excitement in the bombardment was pleasing."

Almería is close enough to the wild region of the Alpujarras to have a number of fantastic stories of the people of those mountains, and indeed Spain has always been a place of dramatic life-stories and strange situations. Where else could a man and his mistress travel down to Granada, in order to find new girls for their string of brothels, with no disguise that this was their business? Where else but in Spain would a distinguished surgeon suddenly renounce his profession and the world, repent not only of his sins but of his scientific knowledge and go about, in religious habits, prescribing herbs for the sick, refusing money, and living like a hermit? Spain produces, as England does, a large number of solitaries; the monasteries and nunneries by no means absorb all the disjointed souls, the unwanted spinsters and incarnate bachelors. There was a tale about two old ladies shut up in the big house of a village outside Almería. They were the daughters of a town clerk and of a family which claimed to be of ancient distinction and wealth. In fact their father's office is famous in Spanish cities for its corruption. Town clerks make their fortunes. After his death these two ladies found their money dwindling, and when they became very old, it was not enough for them to afford even the small wages of a servant to get them water from the village fountain, for even the big house of a Spanish village will be without running water. They therefore went out very late in the night so as not to be seen to get the water themselves, and this was the only time they left the house. Illness at last shut one in, and then both. They died of thirst.

I have listened to dozens of tales of family and personal pride, and this story of the daughters of the town clerk does not sound untrue. These life-stories have always some element of human fantasy, extremity, and disorder, such as used to be found in Russian novels. The Civil War produced a crop of miracles where "Communists" were struck dead by the hand of a saint as they went to set fire to an altar, when brothers called to brothers across the Tagus when this river separated the fronts, when fathers were challenged by their bastards.

The story of the siege of the Alcázar at Toledo is well known. The commanding officer refused to surrender and save the life of his son. In all Spanish tales there is fantasy and the primitive extreme. Like the Russia of the nineteenth century—and today—Spain is full of individuals who grow, regardless of society, into their own full, dramatic bloom. Even when the element of truth in the tales told is small, they indicate the extreme dramas the Spaniards like to imagine. But so many strange things can be seen in Spain that one believes everything. I once talked with three blind peasant women near a fork of a deserted country road in the north, who wanted to walk to Vigo and feared they would take the wrong turning to León. "Sir, we are blind," their voices went up. Two were totally blind, the third could see just a little. Gaunt, tall, in their black dresses, splashed by the red mud of the rains, they were going to walk one hundred and fifty miles. They were not beggars or gypsies.

Almería is a byword in Spain for its remoteness, yet its port and its banks are busy and its grapes are famous. It is a small place to look at, yet it has 100,-000 inhabitants: all Spanish towns are bursting with their population. In England such a place might have 20,000 at the most. The poor are as thick as flies in the heat and dust among the cactus of the hills on the outskirts, in the strange chessboard of low Oriental houses of a single storey, those houses one so often sees in the south: colour-washed, with huge heavy

231

doors and iron-grilled windows that seem far too large
for the house. The very poor have their caves in the
steep rock, and they go up to them on rough tracks.
Outside the town are blocks of pleasant, small, new
houses for workers. The Franco regime has built many
of these small estates. That does not mean the housing
of the lowest-paid labourers. It never does in Spain.
There is always that large population just above the
starvation line which lives where and how it can: in
shacks, sheds, and huts along the beaches. Yet here—
such is the force of "the good appearance"—one will
see a very respectably, almost smartly dressed girl
leave one of these shacks where her brothers are playing naked, and where the mother is saying, with a
fatalistic pride: "You see us in our misery"—you will
see this girl leave the place for her job in the ice-cream
bar or the cake stall in the town, and go with a friend
to walk in the evening *paseo*.

At six in the evening the country buses collect their
passengers for the drive back to the villages. A barrel
organ strikes up to entertain the departing, and the departure is more like a family gathering than something
on a schedule. The passengers, their lives and wishes,
the events of arrival or departure, are more important
than the bus, which itself is more like some dusty animal than a machine. The machine, one could say, has
been dominated by the human beings and has not

dehumanized them. If the bus is hot, if one chokes with
dust, if one's teeth are rattled loose and the drive is
hair-raising, subject to breakdowns and disaster, these
horrors are countered by the liveliness of the people.
They live. They look at the bus with contempt. The
"backward" countries have retained the human qualities we are so anxious to lose in the interests of effi-
ciency. It is true that, unlike us, these passengers are
not day-dreamers; they are not imaginative; they are
jumping crackers living in the minute and without
much sense of anything beyond themselves. Their life
is on the surface.

The evening *paseo* in Almería reveals the great
beauty of the women. Many are superb, almost all
are fine. So many beautiful women are there that the
senses are bewildered and quietened; one finds oneself
in a state of exalted contemplation. It is as well: the
women are unapproachable. No glance is ever returned. By nine o'clock they have gone. The only
women to be seen after that are the raucous lottery-
seller, the old gypsy, the fierce girl at the counter, the
bar, or the cake kiosks. The town has come into the
possession of the men once more and in hundreds they
sit about or walk; the male voice, rumbling or shouting, rules the quiet warm night.

The mind drifts to Chekhov in Almería. We are
in one of his bright but fading Black Sea towns.

One feels the shut-in provincial life ruled by habit and dominated by one or two families. I passed a "school": twenty little children packed round a dining-room table in a tiny front room, with the master—rather like Chekhov to look at—jammed against the door. A charming sight; but these were privileged children. They actually had a school to go to. As I sat in one café, I counted twenty blind passers-by in a quarter of an hour, and after that gave up. They are the victims of trachoma. Almería, too, like Málaga was a Red town in the Civil War—all Spanish ports were. The maritime towns, with their sense of the world outside of Spain, have always been republican and liberal, liberal too in their Catholicism—which, according to the catechism in use there still, is mortal sin. The fortress-like Cathedral was untouched, but the Reds burned Santo Domingo with its patron Virgen del Mar. That has been rebuilt inside where the damage was done, and the Virgin in her green cloak looks very pretty in her jewels and her floodlighting. The burning is not to be defended; but the fire burned out the traditional gloom of churches like this. At Mass on Sunday, Santo Domingo was packed out, but clearly by the "good people" as they say—that is to say, the solid, the secure who have a little money. A young priest from Málaga told me: "We have lost the poor—and it is our fault."

Chapter IX

Before running into the town of Murcia itself one can turn off to look at the outer parts of the province, by the sea, where the women of Mojácar veil their faces with shawls, where no rain falls, and where the villages are wretched. The *fondas* are often dirty; one or two have given themselves a coat of whitewash and have cleaned up inside, but the food is scanty, poor, and dear, flies swarm over everything, and the people are morose. In the main cafés of these villages there are no customers, but they swarm with shouting youths and children who run round the tables while the proprietor sits miserably with a friend near the counter, playing cards. A single, dim electric bulb puts a dejected yellow light on the place. Those who work do so chiefly in the agricultural seasons, but not for the rest of the year, and, as usual, one has the impression of two classes: those who are obliged to work themselves to death, and those who idle to their death. A man with a treasure—a lorry, for example—will slave fanatically all through the night, repairing the engine, keeping the whole village awake. A sad region—the end of human hope. A meal will be garlic soup, which is a thin liquid with bread soaked in it, and two or three small fish. The wine is thin and disgusting. Yet this was once the rich mining province of Europe. The wealth of Tyre was founded on the precious metals which the Phœnicians took from Murcia; its mines enabled Hannibal to make war on Rome. The Carthaginian shafts can still be seen. Under the Moors, Murcia was a continuous garden, and was sometimes compared with Egypt. Now the Murcians are the poor outlanders of Spain, marked, as in Almería, by trachoma from the esparto grass, ill-fed, and with a proverbial dislike of themselves.

"El cielo y el suelo es bueno—el entresuelo malo" —heaven and earth are good, but what lies between is bad. The Murcians have the reputation of being "litigious, superstitious, and revengeful."

But one sees how good the earth can be in the *huerta* or oasis of Murcia, where the old irrigation has been maintained. The long mountain walls, levelled at the top, so that one is travelling for tens of miles below an entrenchment of precipices, are the violet, silver, and rust colour of iron ore, but in the plain the dark palms wind in their stately turbaned processions upon the yellow soil. These palms will become thicker until the desert town of Elche is reached. The fig and the orange, the brown soda plant, the silver olives, and the cotton flower grow. In the gardens of the well-watered city of Murcia itself the pomegranate swells, the red chilis are laid out to dry in squares on the slopes by the road. Rabidly the Spaniards who work get what they can out of their land.

The brown city with its low heavy tiled roofs is scattered round its churches and the mass of its Cathedral. In this town one comes across the first decent bookshop for weeks. The main street, covered by awnings against the daily stunning of the sun that flattens the population and makes walking about after eleven in the morning an oppression, recalls, in a more provincial way, the prosperous well-being of Seville. It is pleasant to pass their good shops and their airy cafés, to see the large family groups of the prosperous talking through the cool night. And by family I mean a full gathering of in-laws, and grandparents: one sees how powerful, gay, and quick of tongue are the women in these patriarchal gatherings. Those night conversations of Spain: the enormous family gathers in its circles and there they shout and laugh. Yet there is not always laughter. One can pass the open balcony where another huge group of relatives sits. The head is walking up and down reciting a prayer for the dead, while the rest gravely, in that strange, harsh monotone of which the Spaniards are masters, intone the responses. In these large families who love the fantastic tale or the long, detailed description, the dead are a continual memory. It is the custom in the evening to remember them.

A green river moves slowly past the tropical gardens of the town and past the long dike or promenade which is the walk for families, for lovers, nurses, and for children stiffened by their best clothes. The lovers walk a yard apart, the hands never touch; the children —to an English eye—are vain, passionate, and spoiled. Constantly, because they are in their best clothes, they have to be checked and told not to do this and that; a continuous nervous series of commands goes out to the little anarchists and egotists, who are thereby stimulated very early to defiance, temper, and wilfulness. As long as they preserve "the fine appearance," they can do what they like. Sad, proud, brilliant-eyed, little sallow faces, they already have the national self-regard. In a few years the spoiled boys will be shouting orders to the mothers and women who spoil them.

The Spanish Temper

"Mother!" the youth of eighteen shouts from the other end of the flat. "What?" shouts back the lady. "Come here," he orders. And if she does not come at once, shouts with violence. Obediently the mother goes to the grown son, not the son to the mother.

The people of Murcia seemed to me easy and generous. We went to see Salzillo's carvings at the hermitage on the outskirts of the town, and on our way back, an old lady stopped me to ask me to admire the flowers she had picked, for all these southerners have a child's adoration of flowers. Another made a poetic speech about her pig that was lying in the street.

"Isn't he beautiful, isn't he fat, isn't he lovely? How rich and fine he is! Oh, how lovely, look at him."

These sudden wakings up into spontaneous delight, these sudden leaps out of torpor into pleasure, are the charm of southern character. This woman had a small shop and took me in to see "an even more beautiful pig, a noble one, a fine one," which her sons had just killed. There it was lying on the bench in the small yard by an open forge and a stove, and the sons were shaving off its bristles. Again it was:

"Isn't he lovely? Isn't he fine? Isn't he rich and delicious? I have never seen a pig so beautiful in my life. And there are my two sons, two fine boys, strong, hard-working—a mother never had such sons—who killed the beautiful pig and are getting it ready. And

239

I have put a pot of onions to cook to stuff the pig with, the largest and finest onions from our beautiful garden, and we shall sell the pig, cooked, in slices."

Superlative delight in this big woman's rapturous face. It was, for her, one of those supreme, superlative, hyperbolical moments for which the southerner lives, the crisis of extravagance and delight.

At the hotel the manager was idly doing his books at two in the morning, and reading a Western. A solid intelligent man, he announced loudly that he could see no difference between the Falangists and the Communists—indeed, many of the Communists had notoriously joined the Falange. He was a Socialist of the centre. He had fought for the Republic on many fronts, as a volunteer. "I told them so. They did nothing to me." These manly fellows in all parties are the backbone of Spain: outspoken, immovable, honest, and brave. Many who survived the Spanish War seem to have escaped persecution by sheer force of character. Their difficulty is that, being the energetic element in the country, they are restless. They long to get out of the provincial towns. The man was like the lawyer in Granada, the lorry-driver of Barcelona, the man with a small garage in the small town, restive under his poor money and wanting more scope; and in any case half the population of Murcia wants to leave the province. Spain cannot support its people.

The Spanish Temper

From the Cathedral tower one looks across the town and the oasis, through the clear air, into a Biblical landscape which has the naïve, clear-cut, polished stillness of a lithograph. The candid Mediterranean light is already on the land. The Cathedral is late Gothic, but the delight is in its golden baroque façade. Sacheverell Sitwell has described this façade as one of the best in Europe, and compares it to a piece of cabinet work carved on an immense scale. The green and blue tiled domes of the church and convents of Murcia are marked by statues, and in all parts of the city one comes across the lovely flourishes of that moving and humane mode of art.

The baroque is one of those importations which have been supremely congenial to the Spanish genius and scene. The landscape, whether it is harsh or gentle, calls for this decorative and voluptuous relief. The historians divide Renaissance architecture into four periods (see Martin Briggs's essay on Spanish architecture and sculpture in Allison Peers's *Spain*): the plateresque, the middle Renaissance, the baroque, and the academic revival. The plateresque or goldsmith work can be seen at its best in Salamanca. This casket-like decoration was brought to Spain from Italy by a Catalan goldsmith who settled in Toledo and had a great influence on the Flemish architect Egas, who was one of the great peaceful Flemish invaders. The plateresque is basically Italian, and it proceeds really from the time of Spanish dominion in Italy. There are splendid examples of the plateresque in Valladolid. But the baroque is the mode which most strongly stirred the imagination of the Spanish artists in the seventeenth and eighteenth centuries. They took at once to its formality, its circumstance, its worldliness, which were so happily combined with movement and freedom. In the earlier decades of the seventeenth century, Spain was still in the state of exhaustion that quickly followed the conquests in America; then followed a time of intellectual delight, extravagance, the silver age of the minor artists; and it is this style which Spaniards made their own and which they took to America. Compared with them, the Anglo-Saxon colonists of the north produced no architecture of transcendent interest. They exterminated the Indians and built pleasant homes, but no great buildings. The Spaniards did not exterminate their Indians and built imaginatively. The statues, the broken cornices, the porticoes and pomp of baroque, its suggestion of epicurean balance and energy, are the beginnings of an extravagance which the extreme and fantastic spirit of the Spaniards soon entered upon. Did they have this passion for detailed exuberance from the Moors? Certainly the Cartuja in Granada emulated the Alhambra; and it is to the Moorish tile-makers that Spanish baroque owes its use of the green and blue tiled domes that are characteristic of the style; Valencia is a city of these tiles. The true Spanish excess is seen in the work of Churriguerra and his disciples. Such are the celebrated doorway of the Hospicio Provincial in Madrid, an orgy of decoration which at first seems vulgar—but upon reflection one sees that this bold carving of deep shapes is very suited to the powerful sunlight in which the deep relief has to be seen. These decorations seem to quarry the sunlight, as well as to fantasticate the stone.

After Murcia there are small baroque towns like Villareal de la Plana and Valencia, and in all the towns between them and Alicante the baroque façade meets the eye, delighting by its gaiety, its composure, its assurance of sensuous pleasure on earth. There will be no seeking after God here; He will come to us without disturbance and be a pagan like ourselves and content with a miracle or two. No mystics can be thought of in these amicable convents; the church is a drawing-room, heaven is inlaid mother of pearl. The clergy yawn with a day's indigo growth of bread on their chins and scratch and nudge as they intone their harsh, sonorous and no longer meaningful prayers. Upon the façades of these churches are the gourmet's calm, the hedonism and drama of a civilization that has gone. Golden in the sun, they are ecclesiastical stomachs reposing upon their dozing authority.

Murcia has a reputation for its *pasos*, or images, which are borne round in Holy Weeks. Like other Spanish towns, Murcia considers its *pasos* supreme in Spain, a point one would never dispute with a *murciano*. A pagan scepticism, blowing in from the Mediterranean and touched by Italy and Rome, enlivens the *murcianos*. In fact, the *pasos* really are remarkable. The figures were carved in wood by Salzillo, the last of the great Spanish polychrome artists, of whom Montañés is the chief. The figures are in a hermitage on the outskirts of the town and the outstanding ones are an almost life-size modelling of the Last Supper. Caught to the life by Spanish realism, the disciples sit gesturing at the table as one walks in awe round it. One has intruded upon living people. One almost resents the dramatic expressiveness of the faces; one is meeting, this time in art, the overwhelming and dominant sense of the human personality that the Spaniards convey to one in life. These figures recall so many scenes of public repentance and self-dramatization in Spanish churches and Holy Week processions. The Spanish religious artists get their realism from the dramatic sense of life in the people around them. Hence the pagan familiarity of the people with their religious images, which are admired for their cost, richness, and beauty and are treated with the easy, conversational intimacy, half-mocking, half-reverent, but wholly possessive, one would give to a son, wife, father, or betrothed in the street. The conception of God seems never to be metaphysical, and the spirit cannot be conceived of by them—it would seem—without the flesh. Man is not raised to God, but God is brought down to man. The Spaniards and their God are of the earth, and in the harsh bang of the church bells from the worn, proud churches one is made aware of a peremptory and ubiquitous temporal power, conventional, pedantic, customary. There will be no escape. One will learn fatalism from those intolerable bells.

That long Mediterranean coast from Alicante northwards turns to the richest country in Spain and the most intensively cultivated in Europe. The figs, the olives and vines of Murcia give place to the orange groves of the Levante, glossy in their brigades, and to the rice fields. One good main road only runs to Barcelona; the rest of the roads are either cut into deep ruts by the orange carts or pot-holed by the lorries. In any case, the road disappears in the wide, dusty towns. The car grinds from hole to hole.

The mountains keep out the winds of Castile from this long fertile strip, and in the early spring they are

made snowy by the almond blossom. Above each large
town the mountain spur is crowned by the long castle
walls of the Roman occupation, and in the towns the
oranges are cased, the rice is sacked, the grapes are
brought in for the Valencian market. In towns like
Játiva and Gandía there are large threshing-floors—
for there is little agricultural machinery in Spain—
and the white husks of the maize are set out in orderly
patterns on the pavements. Nothing is wasted in the
Mediterranean. The women sweep the maize into
heaps at their doorsteps, big, large-boned women who
can carry anything on their hips. All this region is a
suburb of Rome. The blue houses look at the blue sea
towards southern Italy, and on the flat roofs the
kindling wood is stacked in its bundles, the pumpkins
ripen, and the tame rabbits run. There are no fields of
grass here and there is no cornland, for this country
depends on its rich irrigated soil, which runs sometimes
to five crops a year like an intensive garden. Outside
and higher up in the mountain there is not much for
a wild rabbit to eat. The tame rabbit goes into the
paella—that dish of rice, oil, meat, fish, and peppers
which, in one form or other, is the main meal of these
places.

Valencia is the province of tiny farms which are
hardly more than gardens. On two acres a man does
well; on ten acres he is rich. It is the old Spanish story:

good rainfall or water and you have the small peasant proprietor or the wine-grower whose lease is determined by the length of life of his vines. The land reverts to the owner when three quarters of the vines have died, which meant (up to the nineties of last century, before the phylloxera fell upon the vines) that a tenant had a good fifty years' run. Since the nineties the vines come from America, and their life is only half as long. Everything on the land is, of course, political, and the rural quarrel about the reduced lease and the American vine has for years been at the back of the revolutionary troubles in this rich region. The people are either plain Left or Right, republican or traditionalist; anticlericalism is strong, Catholicism is liberal rather than reactionary; the anarchists, who were thick along the Mediterranean— many of them migrants from the true home of anarchism in the south—were on the poor dry land. In the Civil War, many a Catholic will tell you proudly, he was Red. The general spirit is the civilized, worldly, pagan, active, hard-working, and sceptical spirit of the Mediterranean basin; the social conscience is strong, but not fanatical. There is deep respect for the older liberal leaders in their exile in France and Majorca.

The fairs and fiestas are gay; the severe spirit of Castile is far away, and though the girls who are

trimming the grapes in the fields will soon tell you—
in one of those characteristic protest meetings that
take place at a moment's notice in any Spanish village
—that they earn only fifteen pesetas a day from
seven till seven (which is only $2.38 a week at the
present rate of exchange), they belong to a traditionally prosperous community. The rice exchange in
Valencia, where the peasants bring their samples to the
desks and cunning men finger the grains in their palms,
is very much a place of peasant sharpness and prosperity. Haggling over small bargains is a Mediterranean
pleasure. A town like Játiva has three cinemas, and at
half past one in the morning, as the audience sits in the
open air, one hears the bawling of its sound track, the
roar of its *cante flamenco*, half-way across the dark
town. In Valencia, which has become a little Madrid
in its central part, the nights are a hell of noise; but
the city is not a typical city of urban civilization.
Everyone has family connections in the villages
around. The bank clerk goes out to his uncle's in the
country to collect his oranges, and with Mediterranean care will treat the fruit as if it were a vintage
wine, going only to a particular orchard, and there to
a few trees which he knows have the delicate flavour
he likes. He is not the pre-war bank clerk, for in order
to keep pace with the cost of living, he takes on extra
work at night, or puts off the retiring age. It is the

tale of the middle classes all over western Europe; they survive at the cost of working two or three times as hard as they used to do.

The sights of Valencia are its Cathedral and its churches and its market, the Longa or exchange in florid and lovely Gothic, and its palaces. They claim to have the Holy Grail in the Cathedral. It is a disappointing object which might have come from Tiffany's. There is a Neapolitan rather than a purely Spanish disengagement about the devout who go into the churches here to kneel and to murmur their prayers. They gaze about them as they pray, or yawn, or wander about waiting for friends; this is more like Italy than Spain. At night there is music in the cafés, mild tunes for the bourgeoisie, rowdier ones for the populace. Valencia is a lively city, but it is also a place of bad memories in the Civil War—the road outside has sinister memorials to the murdered supporters of Franco—for this was the heart of the Republican region and the seat for a long time of the government; on the other hand, such is Spanish intolerance, there are no memorials to the murdered Republicans anywhere in Spain. The thousands massacred in the bull-ring at Badajoz have no remembrance; the bones of the poet García Lorca lie in a pit into which hundreds of anonymous bodies were thrown. (See Gerald Brenan: *The Face of Spain*.)

In this region one notices a change in the attitude to the Civil Guard. The Guards are thick in the pleasure resorts, in places like the pretty town of Benidorm, perhaps because the rich have a passion for protection, perhaps because Benidorm is a very agreeable place. There is no doubt that the very rich Spaniards have had the fright of their lives. In the south, in Andalusia, the Civil Guard is the traditional ally of the bailiff on the large estates, who watches the huge population of serfs; in Valencia, and much more in Catalonia, the Guards keep their eye on a prosperous and predominantly anti-Franco population which, before Franco, always stood for some degree of regional autonomy. The Catalans despise Madrid and poor Castile, and the population does not like this alien armed body who offend the pride of independent and defeated people. The Guards, of course, represent corporate order, solidarity, discipline, and loyalty; whatever may be said against them—and they have behaved at times with great cruelty and are agents of a rotten system—the Spanish state is unimaginable without some such body.

There is moisture in the air along the east coast, and by September one wakes up in the morning to see dirty clouds and sleepy mists all the way down from Barcelona. For miles on either side of Valencia one has run under the heavy shade of plane and acacia, through miles of rich market garden, towards the vineyards of the mouth of the Ebro. Squares of cypress protect the orange groves. The mule carts are packed in the evening with handsome families, all wearing the wide-brimmed straw hat of the region, and a little dog tethered to the axle of the cart trots along behind it, barking. The clouds clear and we are left with the simple eastward face of the Mediterranean sky. It is a coast of promontories and headlands. At Calpe, a monstrous, uninhabited Gibraltar sticks out naked and clear, cut in a massive silver-lavender stare of rock. "Why," says a peasant aggressively, "do people come and gape at it? There are even two hotels. What for? What is the use of it? It isn't beautiful."

"It is strange."

"There is no food on it," he says. "It is just rock. I wish they'd move it away."

Below Tortosa is the promontory of Peniscola, where a small fishing town is built into the ramparts of a castle of the Templars. The blue-washed houses are flat-roofed in the manner of the region, black nets hang over the doors, the streets are made out of rough stone and rock. The place smells of fish, and the village appears to be barnacled onto the precipitous ruins of the castle. I called to a woman at a window that I wanted to get into the castle. She shouted down the street to another house in an iron voice. A loud squawk came out of the door.

"What is it?"

"Tell Aunt Antonia to open the castle."

A shout from that house to another house, out of sight. "Aunt Antonia, someone at the castle."

"Coming," bawled Aunt Antonia.

The village might have been one family in a great kitchen, everyone shouting orders.

Aunt Antonia came coughing up the street, thin, bent, and shrinking in her jersey. She was a woman of about forty, tired, ill, and morose.

There was a fig tree in the castle. "Are they ripe?" she said. "This one is." And snatched at it and put it in her pocket. She knew, one guessed, every one of those figs, depended in some way on their number. There was the anxiety and precision of poverty in her face; not hunger, but that sort of poverty which in Spain makes people watch every item of their small wealth, even if it is only half a dozen figs. She would sell it, not eat it. She looked like one of those coughing, disheartened, and prickly women one meets in Russian stories.

Down in the shacks on the shore they were frying prawns and langoustine; the smell of burning shells was heavy in the little place. In one place a small band of guitarists with a jazz drum had struck up. It was the fiesta week. One or two couples did a slow, awkward dance on the sand with that air of doughy boredom and that sullen determination not to offend public opinion by unseemly gaiety which make the Spaniards seem so English.

In September the great fiestas go on all up the coast. There was a small bullfight at Peniscola, or rather a teasing of the reluctant and sleepy animals in the "ring" that had been rigged up in the ruins of the castle entrance. Farther north in Tortosa, the fiesta was livelier. Coloured lights, flags across the streets, and giant figures stalked about the town to the sound of drum and whistle. Suddenly these staring dolls appeared at street corners followed by two or three children, all day, without special aim, but mocking everyday life with the reminder that this was homely saturnalia. These giants are a reminder that one is really leaving Iberian Spain, and entering a region which is a good deal Provençal. The giant kings and queens were Fernando and Isabella, the Catholic sovereigns who united this part of Spain with Aragón and Castile and so occupied the peninsula. These giants are really the dolls of forgotten political propaganda. Rockets were exploded all through the night, and for hours there was the scrape, scrape, scrape of strolling people. Another sign of the north at Tortosa was a sporting stadium, and the fiesta was being celebrated with an all-in wrestling display. Half the town turned out for it, walking mysteriously in the dust at about midnight to the arc lights of the place. Large numbers of children went to it. I went with a man who ran a small restaurant and his friend, a carpenter. The restaurant-keeper had fought for the Reds in the Civil War and had escaped by boat to France. He was a typical Catalan of his kind: loathed the rest of Spain, said everything south of Tortosa was Africa and gypsies, hated the Church and Franco and was a Catalan nationalist. There was the usual row at the entrance to the ring. The crowd were shouting together in unison, protesting because the sponsors had put up the price of the tickets. This sort of row is very common. But so nervous and touchy are the authorities in Catalonia that they lose their heads at the smallest signs of public criticism. The gates of the stadium were pulled open suddenly and out rushed a dozen armed Civil Guards. The crowd fled at once, the shouting stopped, and the people were, unpleasantly, cowed.

"That is why we hate Franco," the carpenter said. "Police, for the slightest thing."

It is hard to know in all-in wrestling what is spontaneous and what has been arranged. In Tortosa that night, one saw, however, the Iberian style and the excellent opportunities for the display of native temperament. The boastful, strutting, conceited man came on in his beautiful dressing-gown, followed by a resolved, silent, and austere opponent. Naturally the conceited man soon got the worst of it. He was thrown, flung, scissored; soon he began to foul. The crowd booed him. Spanish pride goes mad under ridicule—except in the restraints of the bullring—and presently the conceited fellow sprang away from his seconds who were mopping him in his corner, charged at his opponent in the opposite corner, and tried to hit him over the head with a pail. In another bout, another, bald, bullet-headed man, with a spade beard and long hairy legs, tried to brain the referee with a bottle. The referee, who was a small middle-aged man in neat white flannels, seized some part of the bearded man and tossed him out of the ring into the audience. Raging, the Beard got back and tried again: the same thing happened. The Beard was finally chased through the audience and half round the stadium by his opponent. Several times the Guards removed people who protested. There were good, clean, imperturbable wrestlers in this display, but one saw in their opponents the other side of Spanish stoicism, strength, and courage: the theatrical, the revengeful side. One saw the "Spanish fury" suddenly spring out, and whether it was genuine or calculated acting, it was tremendous and terrifying in its passion. One also saw what I can only call "the murderous speciality." One wrestler was famous all over the region for the hardness of his skull. He could always be defeated by science and calm, but his dreadful aim was to crack heads with his opponent. One crack from that iron head, that human cannon ball, could half kill any man. The carpenter I was with held his forehead half the time during this bout and made whining, expectant sounds of sympathetic pain. The night passed in protests, fouls, and horseplay. Dripping with sweat, the wrestlers were led away by their supporters to be cleaned up in the wasteland behind the seats.

Tortosa was badly damaged in the Civil War, and its riverside houses were destroyed. Now they are rebuilt. "Who lives in those houses now?" "The new rich," said the carpenter as we walked back through the soft, black, warm night over the new bridge that has been built over the Ebro.

He was a small bourgeois. His children went to school, he was a respectable man on the European model, questioning, active, and with a good notion of the world beyond the Pyrenees and marked by the toleration and curiosity of the Mediterranean. In Castile, in Andalusia—in what is called Spain—he would have been poor, sombre, hostile to Europe, his children going very little to school. It is a difference of race and temperament; also a difference that arises between life in a rich region and life in a poor one.

Chapter X

At Tarragona one strikes the rock and mountain again, the country dries and rises. It is all mountain between here and the frontier, a hundred or more miles away, and packed, prosperous yellow towns. One learns to put a slice of lemon in the red wine. One eats the best fish in Europe, above all the best shellfish; meals are delicate, long, gluttonous, stretching far into the afternoon. One sees the full, round, lively faces. One sees big, comely, well-fed people. One has forgotten the lean bodies of Castile and sees only the happy composure of the flesh. This comeliness is not like the torpid obesity of Seville, for in Catalonia the fat people are electrified by vitality and energy. They talk loudly, boast at large. I lunched with a wine traveller in Barcelona at one of the small, cheap popular restaurants, in the terrible slum of the Barrio Chino, and as we filled and refilled ourselves, he pointed to the classical figure of the young waitress, a creature divine in her amplitude. *"Doña Abundancia,"* he said with the gourmand's sad, sly sigh.

A *corniche* road winds along the promontories to Barcelona. The beaches are hot and spongy to the feet, the sand burns, and the eyes cannot face the flash of the hot sea. The swimmer finds the waves short, sharp, and violent, each small wave punching like a fist. The scrub seems to smoulder on the cement-coloured soil and rock. One stops in little flat-roofed resorts like Sitges where, in the sudden enthusiastic manner of these people, they put up a small statue to El Greco a few years ago. What the Catalans like, they boost exuberantly. El Greco has nothing to do with Catalonia, but a few people in Sitges who admired him could not resist the notion of doing something publicly about it. The Catalan lives artwardly. If there is fantasy in his head, he wants at once to turn it into commerce, into action, into stone.

Barcelona is a Spanish city, but in spite of itself. Its boulevards, the Ramblas, are French in style; the name comes from the Arabic. The common language is Catalan, which is a form of Provençal. The temperament of the people is energetic, boastful, commercial. The city is a place of big-chinned world-shakers who talk in thousands and millions, of go-getters with briefcases. "It doesn't matter how good-looking you are here," said an astonished Andalusian lorry-driver, "the women won't nibble till they have seen your pocketbook." The province of Catalonia is a mountainous buttress of the Pyrenees, but it is well watered and fertile; its agriculture prospers in innumerable small tenant farms; and Barcelona itself is a great textile manufactory. With Bilbao it is the only industrial city of any account in Spain, and it is an important port. The Barcelonese have tried to claim that Columbus was a native of the city and not of Genoa, and they have built a monstrous statue to him at the bottom of the Ramblas. Unfortunately there is little doubt that Columbus was a native of Genoa; his very avarice proves it.

Modern Barcelona, like Madrid, belongs to the megalomaniac group of northern Mediterranean cities: it has the characteristics of Milan, Genoa, and Marseille, ancient cities to which modern industrialism has come late and suddenly. Immense wealth has gone into the hands of a pushing middle class which still has connections with the peasantry, and this wealth has acted like a series of crude electric shocks upon their minds. They have gone in for fantastic and bombastic architecture. The poor of other provinces have crowded into the bursting city, and it is a horrifying mixture of vulgar splendour and swarming slums. The drying wind from the Pyrenees gives a hard clarity to the air, so that each building when one looks down on it from a height seems separate and has the isolation and hardness of a thing seen in a stereoscope. The thousands of windows stare back like the loopholes of armoured cars, and this distinctness is an assault on the eyes and makes its contribution to what the newspaper headlines have been telling us for more than two generations now: that Barcelona is one of the violent cities of Europe. It looks it.

The tension is political. It is true that the Civil War has exhausted the political movements of Catalonia. The only evidence of the ferment now is the pursuit of revolutionaries turned brigand in the Pyrenees, or the trial of anarcho-syndicalist plotters who have courageously come over the border from Perpignan. If Catalonia is apathetic now, and if men over the age of forty look back with nostalgia to the days of active intellectual life and liberal progress before the Civil War, the fundamental causes of tension in Catalonia still exist and will continue to do so for a long time. For though Catalonia likes to regard its separateness from the rest of Spain as its own personal problem, the fact is that Catalonia embodies the struggle between Europe and Iberia (not to say Africa) in the Spanish heart, and in the most active and concrete form. Catalonia is the one part of Spain which has successfully made itself Western and where the balance is tipped in favour of Europe.

In Castile, the unifying principle, despotic, aristocratic, conservative, frugal, tragic: in Castile the mediæval spirit, Don Quixote defeated, Sancho Panza in office and dominant. Castile, the *rentier;* Catalonia, the maker. In Castile, wheat; in Catalonia, cloth. In Catalonia, industrial society, middle-class, optimistic, liberal, sceptical, and very anticlerical in religion, but split violently by the class wars of industrial society. Modern capitalism entered Spain in the forties of last century when foreign companies came in to build the railways. The only peoples to vie with the foreigners were the new Basque iron-founders and bankers and the textile-manufacturers of Barcelona. The attraction of Spain to the northerner is its rejection of modern life, its refusal of the Reformation, the French Revolution, of all that we call Progress; this rejection is not entirely negative by any means. By indolence and recalcitrance the Spaniards have preserved their individuality, a creature unashamedly himself, whose only notion of social obligation is what old custom dictates. The Spaniards have demonstrated that people can survive as personalities without good government, without a sense of corporate responsibility, without compromise, without tolerance—and that, in being themselves, they are willing to pay the appalling social price which their negligence exacts. They are not unnerved by having to face the worst every day; so long as once, every decade or so, they can break out in destructive rage against one another.

Barcelona has stood against this spirit. In practical terms, since 1840 its people have created the only solid middle class in Spain, whose role, according to the historians, was to facilitate the emergence from the mediæval system when it broke down. Catalonia could have Europeanized Spain, but failed to do so, in one major crisis after another, because its political separatism made it suspect to Madrid. The differences between the Spanish regions are not merely picturesque; they are real and strong, and in the nineteenth and early twentieth centuries, the Catalans were deeply separated from Madrid. To such an extent that the Madrid government actually employed police agents to assassinate rich employers in Barcelona after the rising in 1909. That is to say, the Madrid police used the workers' revolutionary movements in Barcelona against the employers in order to teach Catalan nationalism a lesson.

In 1909 Catalonia had risen to stop Catalan reservists

being sent to the unpopular Moroccan War. In all the violent strikes, street wars, bomb-throwings, and *coups d'état* of Barcelona, this particular one is instructive in its simple illustration of what happens in Spain after acts of revolt. The rising was crushed. It brought changes in Madrid. But the outstanding scapegoat was a man who had had nothing to do with the revolt: the schoolteacher Ferrer, whose name became world-famous as one of the martyrs of liberty. As so often happens, not a martyr whom all liberals found entirely acceptable. But whatever the character of Ferrer was, the real reason for his execution was that he was an atheist who conducted a free school, outside of the clerical monopoly; he was shot at the request of the clerical party. Ferrer was only one of the many founders of free schools in Spain, and he was certainly not a great man. The great name in modern Spanish education, as I have said earlier, was Francisco Giner de los Ríos, who was one of those who influenced a whole generation and played an important part in the intellectual renaissance which made Madrid a brilliant place before 1936. The execution of Ferrer did not in fact kill the free-school movement, but it showed the political power of the Church and its sense of what was the vital political question. Once more in the exhaustion after the Civil War the Church is the real political victor, not General Franco. The first movement to go was the movement for "free schools." The free schools were, of course, far from being atheistical in the crude manner of Ferrer; indeed, they were attended chiefly by the children of sound Catholic families, who thought official Catholic education inferior and out of date. Few except the extremists among the believers think it good.

The political situation in Barcelona has always been complicated by the issue of Catalan nationalism. At first this movement was in the hands of the rich manufacturers, and when these men were pacified by government office and by tariffs, it fell into the hands of the lesser middle classes and the workers. But the chief revolutionary force was the anarcho-syndicalists. I need not describe the rise of this party in Spain nor its actions in Barcelona before and during the Spanish Civil War, but it is necessary to add to what I have already said about the movement. Anarchism was, essentially, a protest against industrial capitalism itself, by people who lived in an old, pre-industrial, mediæval culture. When workers and peasants saw the Church allying itself with the industrial order, they lost their faith, and anarchism became a religion. It was preferred to Communism and Socialism because it was not materialistic, because it rejected industrial capitalism altogether and regarded the whole system as morally corrupting.

The Spanish Temper

In *The Spanish Cockpit*, Borkenau says:

Anarchism is a religious movement, in a sense profoundly different from the sense in which that is true of the labour movements of the progressive countries. Anarchism does not believe in the creation of a new world through the improvement of the material conditions of the lower classes, but in the creation of a new world out of the moral resurrection of those classes which have not yet been contaminated by the spirit of mammon and greed. At the same time anarchism is far from being well-behaved and pacifist; it has integrated, in its mentality, all the Robin Hood tradition of former generations and emphatically believes in violence; not in organised conflict only, but in fighting as an everyday means of settling the divergence of views between simple men and their masters. . . .

A notable number of criminals were admittedly in the anarchist ranks, and the anarchists were indeed responsible for robberies, casual shootings, and church-burnings in the Civil War. The anarchists were intolerable to the European Left-wing participants in the Civil War, and were uncontrollable. But Catalans who supported Franco have told me that the Chekas, or Communist-run secret courts in Catalonia, were loathed because they "killed behind closed doors, coldly, after trial." This "deeply offended the Catalan nature and tradition," which is to shoot suddenly, in hot blood, publicly, in the street. An example of hot-blooded attack by anarchists was the burning of the notorious Women's Prison in Barcelona, where generations of workers had seen their wives and daughters taken. It was an act rising from generations of indignation. The Communists—as Mr. Langdon-Davies notes in his excellent book on Catalonia, *Gatherings in Catalonia*—would have built a better prison: the exalted anarchists would have had no prison at all. The tension in Barcelona is primitive; it can be compared with the tension in the north of England at the time of the Chartist risings. It is a primitive protest against the satanic mills. Now, since 1939, Barcelona is quiet; thousands of Reds must have joined the Franco Falange. One has, all the same, the impression that, in time, the old pattern of Barcelona politics will reappear.

The only reason for thinking the revolutionary situation closed is that Europe has certainly moved out of that revolutionary state of mind which dominated it between the two wars. Perhaps a process of adjustment has been completed; intellectual and political ferment has certainly gone.

The modern city of Barcelona, north of the Plaza de Cataluña, is a piece of grandiose planning. Wide boulevards make the long climb towards the mountains. There are *rond-points* like deserts at the intersections; the city has been built for a motor age that has not seriously arrived in Spain. There are no Spanish manufacturers of motor-cars. In the Paseo de Gracia there are blocks of flats built by the fantastic school of architects who thrived at the beginning of the century, very much under the influence of Art Nouveau. The lines of these buildings are wavy in heavy shallow curves and suggest, rather disagreeably, a style based on over-succulent and pulpy tropical vegetation, the hollow stems of the banana, the spongy stem and umbrella of the toadstool. The Germanic note, the suggestion of Grimm's fairy tales turned soft, is obvious. The originality of Gaudí, the outstanding architect of this school, is characteristic of the fantastic side of the Catalan imagination. The chief example of Gaudí's talent—perhaps we should call it visionary genius working in isolation—is the notorious Cathedral of the Sagrada Familia. This neo-Gothic Cathedral is unfinished. There is a façade, there are four towers like factory chimneys made in stone fretwork. Plants, flowers, animals, dominate the detail of the façade. A cypress shelters a doorway; stone leaves, like creepers or vines, trail over the design. A rose breaks open, a capital bursts into palm leaves, ornate fruits, phallic buds, and abstract pods appear on pinnacles, a cape of snow-laden pine branches—or so it appears—encloses the Puerta de la Fe, trees and jewelled canopies envelop corners, a flamingo grows out of a pillar as if it were being drawn out of dough by the fingers of a skilled confectioner. Certainly the Cathedral celebrates the riot of nature romantically, decoratively, and with a studied determination to break every architectural convention. Although the mood is Gothic, the gorging of decoration is baroque and one's mind goes back to the excesses of Churriguerra; all the more as one learns that Gaudí felt that he was creating a hymn to life, and that the essence of life was colour. A great deal of what is now grey and doughy stone would have been a glitter of jewelled vermilions, greens, and blues—which once more suggests the fantasies of the pastry cook, but also reminds us of the Spanish taste for polychrome statuary and the tiled domes of the churches in Valencia. The hard, clear, serene Mediterranean light can assimilate colour. All the layman can say of the Sagrada Familia is that some of its original detail is strong and exciting, and some flaccid, feeble, and sick-spirited. We are really looking at a fragment of a building which the architect decided to turn inside out. And as we go away, we can reflect that the taste for the bizarre, for the multiform, the over-decorated, the impulse to excess, is very Spanish. Before the war one could compare the excess of riotous baroque in the Church of Belén on the Ramblas with the Sagrada Familia, but Belén was burned out in the Civil War and now has a severe classical austerity. The anarchists—as Mr. Langdon-Davies says—liked baroque because it burned. The excess of Barcelona, the excess of Gaudí, the excess of Dali, the excess of Picasso—half Catalan, half *malagueño*—is native.

The city is dominated by the mountain called Tibidabo and the repellent church that is being built on its summit. One would a thousand times sooner have Gaudí's work than this religious Odeon. The building has been going on for a generation, and a terrible figure of the Christ stands in the courtyard waiting to be heaved on top, where its halo will be electrically lit. The collapse of Spanish religious art has this awful monument, which is one of the jokes of the city.

One of the world-shakers who showed me round Barcelona again stopped in the street and pointed to this horror. "Through that building," he said, "I lost my religious faith. For it was announced on a public notice when I was young that by Divine Promise the church would be completed by a certain date that was named. It was not completed, and I complained to one of the fathers, who explained that by completion was meant that the roof would be on. That was too much for me." Oh blessed, pagan, literal Mediterranean. With worldly eye you regard those offers of indulgences inscribed on the walls of Tibidabo. Childishly you take your families for a joy ride at the Amusement

Park, which has been placed beside the church on the precipice overlooking the city. Savagely you drove your political prisoners there, only fifteen years ago, on the last ride of their lives, gave them the last cigarette, and shot them.

Long before we reached the city, at a second crossing of the Ebro by some bad mountain road, we came to a new steel bridge across this superb river. Green and smooth as marble, or thick blood-colour, according to the season, it is a river that flows a good deal in profound ravines, as indeed do most of the Spanish rivers. We crossed the bridge and stopped for a glass of beer on the other side. There were four men in the café playing cards, and I asked the proprietor which side had destroyed the bridge in the Civil War. He was a dusty, thin-haired, sly-faced man in his fifties.

"The others," he said.

"But who are the others?" I said. "Fascists or the Reds?"

"The others," he said. "In a civil war," he said, "it is always 'the others'—and whoever wins is right."

And saying this, he rubbed his forefinger lightly down his nose and let it rest at the tip—the gesture of innuendo, the gesture of Sancho Panza. One will find the correlative passage in almost any chapter of that book, which contains all other books on Spain.

Index

Index

Index

Index